GRAMMAIRE ECLAIR

by Graeme S.F. Kirk, M.A. (Oxon)

Target Language Consultant: Marie-Neige Smith

First published 1996 by Senlac Language Publications,
P.O. Box 94, St Leonards-on-Sea, East Sussex TN37 7ZW.

Also available by the same author:
<u>Vocabulaire Eclair</u> ISBN 0 9527931 3 X
<u>Grammatik ohne Panik</u> ISBN 0 9527931 0 5
<u>Vokabeln ohne Panik</u> ISBN 0 9527931 2 1

To order more copies of this booklet or any of the others above,
please photocopy the form on the inside back cover.

Printed by Scarbutts Ltd,
West Malling, Kent

ISBN 0 9527931 1 3

CONTENTS

GRAMMAIRE ECLAIR

Why Grammar?

If you don't learn the rules of a game, you can't win: if you don't learn the rules of a language, you won't be able to use it for your own purposes. 'Grammar' is just a word for the rules of the language. Work hard at developing your understanding of grammar, and French will be more fun.

The Explanations

The aim is to explain each point as briefly and clearly as possible. Although we try to keep the language simple, we do use words like noun, verb and adjective, explaining them as we go along.

The Exercises

The aims are to get you to practise the grammar points in a variety of ways, as a relatively painless way of learning them, and to make sure you know how to use them. The exercises include gap filling, putting words in the right order and translation: it's not much use being able to construct fancy sentences in French if you don't know what they mean! A lot of the vocabulary you're asked to use is either basic and familiar or is explained, but a good dictionary is always useful.

The GCSE / Standard Grade Exam

The GCSE / Standard Grade Exam encourages communication, so don't be put off if you make some mistakes. But you are required to understand some basic grammar, and working through this book should help you get a higher grade.

Bonne chance!

KEY TO INSTRUCTIONS FOR EXERCISES

dans le bon ordre	-	in the right order
la bonne réponse	-	the right answer
chaque question	-	each question
comment ça se dit?	-	how do you say that?
le contraire de	-	the opposite of
déchiffre	-	decipher
en dessous de	-	below
écris les réponses	-	write the answers
mets	-	put
en mots	-	in words
les mots soulignés	-	the words underlined
la phrase	-	the sentence, phrase
Qui avait fait ça?	-	Who had done that?
relie	-	join up
remplace par	-	replace with
remplis les blancs	-	fill in the blanks
réponds	-	answer
réussir aux examens	-	to pass the exams
sers-toi de ...	-	use ....
s'il le faut	-	if necessary
traduis	-	translate
trouve	-	find
voici les réponses	-	here are the answers
..... vont ensemble	-	..... go together

GRAMMATICAL TERMS

l'adjectif	-	adjective
le conditionnel	-	Conditional Tense
la conjonction	-	conjunction
le féminin	-	feminine
le futur	-	Future Tense
l'imparfait	-	Imperfect Tense
l'impératif	-	Imperative
le masculin	-	masculine
le négatif	-	negative
le nombre	-	number
le participe passé	-	past participle
le passé composé	-	Perfect Tense
le pluriel	-	plural
le plus-que-parfait	-	Pluperfect Tense
la préposition	-	preposition
le présent	-	Present Tense
le pronom	-	pronoun
le substantif	-	noun
le verbe (ir)régulier	-	(ir)regular verb

NOUNS AND GENDER (1)

What is a noun?

A noun is the name of a person, object, place or idea,

e.g.:	bateau	-	boat	gare	-	station
	personne	-	person	bonheur	-	happiness

Most dictionaries show that a word is a noun by putting the letter 'n' after the word.

What is a gender?

In French, nouns can be divided into two groups: masculine or feminine. These are known as genders. You can find out the gender of a noun by using a dictionary or referring to a word list. Most dictionaries show that a word is masculine or feminine by putting 'm' or 'f' after the 'n' for noun,

e.g.:	prénom nm	-	first name	natation nf	-	swimming
	argent nm	-	money	tante nf	-	aunt

It is easier in the long run to learn the gender of a noun at the same time as you learn the noun itself.

EXERCICES

A Substantif: oui ou non?
Sers-toi d'un dictionnaire.

1 pantoufle
2 arc-en-ciel
3 arranger
4 près
5 manège
6 juste
7 flèche
8 miel
9 siffler
10 gentil

B Masculin ou féminin?
Sers-toi d'un dictionnaire.

1 chaussette
2 nez
3 coca
4 athlétisme
5 pomme
6 porc
7 boulangerie
8 cheville
9 chocolat
10 jupe

FLASH-INFO

You are allowed to use a dictionary in many new exams. Before you buy one, it is a good idea to ask your teacher what sort is recommended by the exam board.

NOUNS AND GENDER (2)

Some Simple Rules

If you don't have a dictionary and you haven't learnt the gender of a noun, there are ways of getting it right most of the time.

1 Telling the gender of a noun by its meaning.

Masculine

a)	Males are generally masculine, e.g.:	homme (nm)	-	man
	Exceptions, e.g.:	*vedette (nf)*	-	*star (entertainment)*
		victime (nf)	-	*victim*
b)	Seasons, e.g.:	automne (nm)	-	autumn
c)	Months, e.g.:	avril (nm)	-	April
d)	Days of the week, e.g.:	lundi (nm)	-	Monday
e)	Points of the compass, e.g.:	sud (nm)	-	south
f)	Trees, e.g.:	chêne (nm)	-	oak
g)	Metals, e.g.:	or (nm)	-	gold

Feminine

a)	Females are generally feminine, e.g.:	mère (nf)	-	mother
b)	Names of countries, e.g.:	France (nf)	-	France
	Exceptions, e.g.:	*Maroc (nm)*	-	*Morocco*
		Portugal (nm)	-	*Portugal*
		Canada (nm)	-	*Canada*
c)	Names of rivers ending in -e, e.g.:	Seine (nf)	-	Seine
	Exceptions, e.g.:	*Rhône (nm)*	-	*Rhone*

2 Telling the gender of a noun by what it looks like.

There are a number of quite complicated rules about the endings of words. It is not helpful to give all the exceptions at this stage, but here are the main endings to look for. If you can only manage one rule, it helps to know that MOST nouns in French which end in -e are feminine. But there are many exceptions to this rule, and to all the others below!

Masculine

a)	Nouns ending in -age, e.g.:	voyage (nm)	-	journey
b)	Nouns ending in -ail, e.g.:	travail (nm)	-	work
c)	Nouns ending in -al, e.g.:	cheval (nm)	-	horse
d)	Nouns ending in -eau, e.g.:	bateau (nm)	-	boat
e)	Nouns ending in -ège, e.g.:	collège (nm)	-	school
f)	Nouns ending in -ent, e.g.:	argent (nm)	-	money
g)	Nouns ending in -et, e.g.:	carnet (nm)	-	book of tickets
h)	Nouns ending in -eur, e.g.:	travailleur (nm)	-	worker
i)	Nouns ending in -ier, e.g.:	panier (nm)	-	basket
j)	Nouns ending in -isme, e.g.:	tourisme (nm)	-	tourism
k)	Nouns ending in -ment, e.g.:	monument (nm)	-	monument
l)	Nouns ending in -on, e.g.:	bâton (nm)	-	stick
m)	Nouns ending in -oir, e.g.:	miroir (nm)	-	mirror

Feminine

a)	Nouns ending in -ade, e.g.:	promenade nf	-	walk
b)	Nouns ending in -aille, e.g.:	bataille nf	-	battle
c)	Nouns ending in -aison, e.g.:	comparaison nf	-	comparison
d)	Nouns ending in -aine, e.g.:	vingtaine nf	-	about twenty
e)	Nouns ending in -ance, e.g.:	distance nf	-	distance
f)	Nouns ending in -çon, e.g.:	leçon nf	-	lesson
g)	Nouns ending in -elle, e.g.:	jumelle nf	-	twin (female)
h)	Nouns ending in -ence, e.g.:	essence nf	-	petrol
i)	Nouns ending in -esse, e.g.:	promesse nf	-	promise
j)	Nouns ending in -ette, e.g.:	crevette nf	-	prawn
k)	Nouns ending in -ion, e.g.:	télévision nf	-	television
l)	Nouns ending in -ise, e.g.:	chemise nf	-	shirt
m)	Nouns ending in -son, e.g.:	maison nf	-	house
n)	Nouns ending in -té, e.g.:	liberté nf	-	freedom
o)	Nouns ending in -tié, e.g.:	amitié nf	-	friendship
p)	Nouns ending in -tie, e.g.:	partie nf	-	part

EXERCICES

A Masculin ou féminin?

1	saule	-	willow	11	mardi	-	Tuesday
2	printemps	-	spring	12	Angleterre	-	England
3	professeur	-	teacher	13	tante	-	aunt
4	hiver	-	winter	14	été	-	summer
5	Tamise	-	Thames	15	Ecosse	-	Scotland
6	soeur	-	sister	16	mécanicien	-	mechanic
7	nord	-	north	17	secrétaire	-	secretary
8	maçon	-	bricklayer	18	décembre	-	December
9	Italie	-	Italy	19	fer	-	iron
10	argent	-	silver	20	vendeur	-	salesman

B Masculin ou féminin?

1	journal	11	ordinateur
2	manteau	12	vitesse
3	maquillage	13	égalité
4	pantalon	14	boisson
5	parent	15	circulation
6	mobylette	16	métier
7	renseignement	17	poulet
8	valise	18	organisation
9	vaisselle	19	château
10	serviette	20	couloir

FLASH-INFO

Some people learn best by listening to themselves on cassette.
They record vocabulary, or passages of writing, or practise speaking tests, and then listen to them on a walkman, or in the car.
Above all, find out what works for you and keep doing it!

PLURALS

When we talk about **more than one** person, object, place or idea (noun), we are using the plural. In English, nouns usually add an 's' in the plural, e.g.: Smiths, rulers, regions, ages.
Some exceptions: children, mice

In French the rule is the same: most nouns add an 's',
e.g.: verre - glass verres - glasses
There are, however, more exceptions to remember:

1 If a noun already ends in '-s', '-x' or '-z', it does not change in the plural,
e.g.: fils - son(s) prix - prize(s), price(s) nez - nose(s)

2 Many nouns ending in '-ail', '-al', '-eu', '-eau' and '-ou' add '-x' in the plural,

e.g.:	travail* >	travaux	-	work(s)
	cheval** >	chevaux	-	horse(s)
	tableau >	tableaux	-	painting(s)
	cheveu >	cheveux	-	hair(s)
	genou >	genoux	-	knee(s)

* note that '-ail' changes to '-aux'.
** note that '-al' changes to '-aux'.

Note
The following are exceptions to the above rule:

bal	> bals	-	dance(s)	festival	> festivals	-	festival(s)
détail	> détails	-	detail(s)	pneu	> pneus	-	tyre(s)
clou	> clous	-	nail(s)	cou	> cous	-	neck(s)
trou	> trous	-	hole(s)				

3 Miscellaneous exceptions:

monsieur	> **mes**sieurs	-	Mr/gentleman > gentlemen
madame	> **mes**dames	-	Mrs/Ms/lady > ladies
mademoiselle	> **mes**demoiselles	-	Miss(es)
oeil	> yeux	-	eye(s)

4 Plural of compound nouns (nouns made up of two parts). One, both or neither part may add an 's'. Use a dictionary to be certain!

e.g.:	timbre-poste	> timbres-poste	-	stamp(s)
	grand-père	> grands-pères	-	grandfather(s)
	porte-monnaie	> porte-monnaie	-	purse(s)

EXERCICE

A Mets les substantifs au pluriel:

1 journal	6 bijou	11 cou	16 colis
2 clé	7 château	12 chou	17 voix
3 détail	8 grand-mère	13 cheval	18 pneu
4 succès	9 tire-bouchon	14 crime	19 trou
5 oeil	10 mois	15 crocodile	20 grand-parent

THE DEFINITE ARTICLE

What is it?

In English, the definite article is '**the**'. Whilst our language uses only one word, in French there are four variations:

le is used with masculine nouns, e.g.:	le garçon	-	the boy
la is used with feminine nouns, e.g.:	la fille	-	the girl
l' is used with masculine and feminine nouns starting with a vowel, e.g.:	l'argent	-	the money
and words beginning with a silent 'h', e.g.:	l'hôtel	-	the hotel
les is used with all plural nouns, e.g.:	les vacances	-	the holidays

THE INDEFINITE ARTICLE

What is it?

In English, the indefinite article is '**a(n)**' in the singular and '**some**' in the plural. In French, the indefinite article is as follows:

un is used with masculine nouns, e.g.:	un garçon	-	a boy
une is used with feminine nouns, e.g.:	une fille	-	a girl
des is used with all plural nouns, e.g.:	des garçons	-	some boys

EXERCICE

A Comment ça se dit en français?
Sers-toi d'un dictionnaire.

1 a river (... rivi...)
2 the cars (... voit....)
3 the sea (... me....)
4 an exercise book (... cah....)
5 the computer (... ordi....)
6 an armchair (... faut....)
7 the cheeses (... from....)
8 the timetable (... hor....)
9 the stories (... his....)
10 a raincoat (... imp....)
11 some men (... ho....)
12 some cars (... voit....)
13 the hospital (... hôp....)
14 a person (... pers....)
15 some people (... ge....)

FLASH-INFO

A dictionary is only as good as its user: avoid both dictionaries for advanced students and micro-dictionaries. A dictionary with about 50,000 references is large enough.

ADJECTIVES

What are they?
Adjectives are describing words,
e.g.: vert - green élégant - elegant confortable - comfortable

How do they change?
In English, they don't change, whatever they are describing,
e.g.: an **elegant** man, an **elegant** woman, **elegant** men, **elegant** women
But in French they add -e if the noun is feminine, -s if it is plural, and -es if it is both feminine and plural,
e.g.: un homme **élégant**, une femme **élégante**, des hommes **élégants**, des femmes **élégantes**
We say that the adjective **agrees** with the noun it describes.

Irregular Adjectives
1 Adjectives already ending in '-e' do not add another 'e' in the feminine,
e.g.: Je porte un pullover jaune et une jupe jaune. - I am wearing a yellow pullover and a yellow skirt.

2 The following common adjectives do not follow the regular pattern and should be learnt carefully:

Masculine Singular	Feminine Singular	Masculine Plural	Feminine Plural	Meaning
ancien	ancienne	anciens	anciennes	ancient / old / former
beau / bel*	belle	beaux	belles	beautiful
blanc	blanche	blancs	blanches	white
bon	bonne	bons	bonnes	good
cher	chère	chers	chères	dear / expensive
doux	douce	doux	douces	mild
faux	fausse	faux	fausses	false / wrong
favori	favorite	favoris	favorites	favourite
frais	fraîche	frais	fraîches	fresh
gentil	gentille	gentils	gentilles	kind
gras	grasse	gras	grasses	fat
gros	grosse	gros	grosses	fat
heureux	heureuse	heureux	heureuses	happy
long	longue	longs	longues	long
mignon	mignonne	mignons	mignonnes	good-looking / sweet
neuf	neuve	neufs	neuves	new
nouveau / nouvel*	nouvelle	nouveaux	nouvelles	new
vieux / vieil*	vieille	vieux	vieilles	old

*This form is used before a noun beginning with a vowel or a silent 'h',
e.g.: Le nouvel élève est arrivé. - The new pupil has arrived.
C'est un bel hôtel! - It's a beautiful hotel!

Position of Adjectives

In French, most adjectives follow the noun they describe,

e.g.: une voiture **blanche** - a **white** car   un garçon **intelligent** - a **clever** boy

However, the following common adjectives come before the noun:

beau	beautiful, nice	joli	pretty
bon	good	long	long
dernier	last	mauvais	bad
gentil	kind	nouveau	new
grand	big, tall	petit	small
gros	fat	premier	first
haut	tall, high	vieux	old
jeune	young		

Note

1 When more than one adjective describes a noun, the same rules apply,
e.g.: un **bon** vin **français** - a **good French** wine

2 A few adjectives come sometimes before and sometimes after the noun according to their meaning,
e.g.: mon **ancien** professeur d'anglais - my **former** English teacher
des maisons **anciennes** - **old** houses
ma **propre** chambre - my **own** room
ma chambre **propre** - my **clean** room

EXERCICES

A Change les adjectifs **s'il le faut**:

1 un **vieux** ordinateur
2 deux **grand** enfants (nm)
3 des filles **intelligent**
4 un monsieur **riche**
5 une fleur **rose**
6 une mère **content**
7 Mon grand-père est **triste**.
8 Elle est **fatigué**.
9 Les vélos (nm) sont **jaune**.
10 Mes cheveux (nm) sont **long**.
11 Le garçon est **gentil**.
12 La femme est **beau**.
13 La table est **blanc**.
14 Ma soeur est **heureux**.
15 Le stylo est **neuf**.
16 Les fraises (nf) sont **frais**.
17 Ma matière **favori**.
18 Un **vieux** homme.
19 Les réponses (nf) sont **faux**.
20 La souris est **mignon**.

B Traduis les phrases de l'exercice **A** en anglais.

C Traduis en français:

1 a large bicycle
2 My hair is short.
3 my favourite pen
4 my own computer
5 a kind mother
6 rich girls
7 a small boy
8 My answer is too long.
9 I am tired.
10 my last question

D Anagrammes:

1 enu nobne diée
2 neu leble aronge
3 nu rgand navio
4 enu motaet uorge
5 nu cas urbn

POSSESSION
(1) Possessive Adjectives

English and French both have ways of saying that people, places or ideas **belong to** different people. One way of doing this is by using a possessive adjective,

e.g.: **mon** livre - **my** book

Ordinary adjectives must agree with the noun (that is, they must add an 'e' if the noun is feminine and / or an 's' if it is plural). Possessive adjectives also agree, but they change in the following ways:

Masculine Singular	Feminine Singular	Plural	Meaning
mon*	ma	mes	my
ton*	ta	tes	your
son*	sa	ses	his / her
notre	notre	nos	our
votre	votre	vos	your
leur	leur	leurs	their

e.g.: **Ma** mère, **leur** frère et **tes** parents arrivent. - My mother, their brother and your parents are arriving.

* These words are also used before any singular noun which begins with a vowel or a silent 'h',

e.g.: Je mets les robes dans **mon** armoire. - I'm putting the dresses in my wardrobe.

Important Note

'**son** cheval' can mean his or her horse: **son** is used because 'cheval' is masculine and not because it belongs to a male person. Similarly '**sa** chemise' can mean his or her shirt: 'chemise' is feminine.

EXTRA-EXTRA-EXTRA-EXTRA-EXTRA-EXTRA-EXTRA-EXTRA-EXTRA-EXTRA-EXTRA-EXTRA-EXTRA

Saying 'mine' in French

One way of expressing 'mine', etc. is to use 'à' + emphatic pronoun (see page 46),

e.g.: Ce stylo est **à moi**. - This pen is **mine**. (literally, 'to me')

Another way is to use '**le mien / la mienne / les miens / les miennes**',

e.g.: Son cheval est blanc, mais **le mien** est noir et blanc. - His / her horse is white, but **mine** is black and white.

Tu as tes livres? J'ai oublié **les miens**. - Have you got your books? I have forgotten **mine**.

EXTRA-EXTRA-EXTRA-EXTRA-EXTRA-EXTRA-EXTRA-EXTRA-EXTRA-EXTRA-EXTRA-EXTRA-EXTRA

EXERCICES

A Traduis en anglais:

1 ma soeur
2 mes frères
3 notre école
4 votre maison (nf)
5 ses tantes
6 ton examen
7 leur salle de bain (nf)
8 sa limonade
9 vos profs
10 mon magasin

B Traduis en français:

1 our shop
2 her brother
3 your sister
4 our exams
5 my bathroom
6 their lemonade
7 your teachers
8 his house
9 my school
10 their aunt

(2) Using 'de' (of)

Another way of saying that someone or something belongs to someone or something else in French is to use **de**,

e.g.:	Voici le frère **de** mon oncle.	- This is my uncle**'s** brother.
	J'ai trouvé l'adresse **des** filles.	- I have found the girl**s'** address.
	Il va acheter le vélo **d'**Eric.	- He is going to buy Eric**'s** bike.
	Qui a vu le livre **du** prof?	- Who has seen the teacher**'s** book?

English uses **s'** and **'s** in the above sentences to show 'belonging', but French never does this. We can understand more easily how the French works if we translate the examples using 'of',

e.g.: This is the brother **of** my uncle.
I have found the address **of the** girls.
He is going to buy the bike **of** Eric.
Who has seen the book **of the** teacher?

French uses **de** to translate 'of', but when it is followed by a word for 'the' in French, the two words sometimes become one word,

that is: de + le = **du**
de + les = **des**
But de + la = **de la**
de + l' = **de l'**

Note
de is shortened to **d'** in front of a vowel or a silent 'h',
e.g.: L'ordinateur d'Anne-Marie est en panne. - Anne-Marie's computer has broken down.

EXERCICES

A Complète les phrases avec **de**, **d'**, **du**, **de la** ou **des**.

1 les enfants ..... ma soeur
2 la voiture ..... Agnès
3 les amis ..... Michel
4 la clé ..... voiture (nf)
5 le maire ..... ville (nf)
6 le directeur ..... collège (nm)
7 les jouets ..... enfants
8 le cartable ..... Paul
9 les questions ..... Monsieur Legrand
10 la capitale ..... Angleterre (nf)

B Traduis les phrases de l'exercice **A** en anglais.

FLASH-INFO

If you learn 10 words twice a week for two years, you will know over 2,000 words!
Learning a little vocabulary thoroughly counts in the end.

DEMONSTRATIVE ADJECTIVES

What are they?
They are the words for **this / that** and **these / those**. These words must agree with the nouns that follow them: that is, they change according to whether the noun which follows is masculine or feminine, and according to whether it is singular or plural.

What are they in French?

	French	Example	Meaning
Masculine Singular noun	ce	ce livre	this / that book
Masculine Singular noun beginning with a vowel or a silent 'h'	cet	cet animal	this / that animal
		cet homme	this / that man
Feminine Singular noun	cette	cette assiette	this / that plate
All Plural nouns	ces	ces garçons	these / those boys

It is clear from the table above that **ce**, **cet** and **cette** can mean both 'this' and 'that'; **ces** can mean both 'these' and 'those',
e.g.: J'ai laissé **ce** livre sur la table. - I left **this** book on the table. or I left **that** book on the table.
Tu as vu **ces** garçons? - Did you see **these** boys? or Did you see **those** boys?

French doesn't usually differentiate between the idea of 'this' and 'that', or between 'these' and 'those', but it can:
e.g.: ce livre-**ci** - **this** book ce livre-**là** - **that** book
ces garçons-**ci** - **these** boys ces garçons-**là** - **those** boys

EXTRA-EXTRA-EXTRA-EXTRA-EXTRA-EXTRA-EXTRA-EXTRA-EXTRA-EXTRA-EXTRA-EXTRA-EXTRA

'this / that / these / those one(s)'
Ce garçon-là est sympa, mais **celui-ci** est désagréable. - That boy is nice, but **this one** is unpleasant.
Cette maison-ci est jolie, mais **celle-là** est laide. - This house is pretty, but **that one** is ugly.
Ces pullovers-ci sont trop grands, mais **ceux-là** sont trop petits. - These pullovers are too big, but **those ones** are too small.
Ces femmes-là sont mariées, mais **celles-ci** sont célibataires. - Those women are married, but **these ones** are single.

'the one / the ones'
Tu préfères quelle robe? Je préfère **celle** à 250 francs. - Which dress do you prefer? I prefer **the one** at 250 francs.
Ceux que j'aime bien s'appellent Martin et Paul. - **The ones** I really like are called Martin and Paul.

EXTRA-EXTRA-EXTRA-EXTRA-EXTRA-EXTRA-EXTRA-EXTRA-EXTRA-EXTRA-EXTRA-EXTRA-EXTRA

EXERCICES

A Remplace **le** / **la** / **l'** / **les** par **ce** / **cet** / **cette** / **ces**

1 le professeur
2 la chambre
3 l'appartement (nm)
4 les étudiantes
5 la langue
6 l'hôtel (nm)
7 les livres
8 le disque compact
9 la cassette
10 l'armoire (nf)

B Anagrammes:

1 vetectalise - this suitcase
2 fsecenants - these children
3 sgsecen - those people
4 ranidectortue - that computer
5 enotectmetr - this watch

NUMBERS

You need these for counting, ages, prices, telling the time, just about everything. Learn them thoroughly!

1	un	21	vingt et un	200	deux cents
2	deux	22	vingt-deux	301	trois cent un
3	trois	30	trente	1 000	mille
4	quatre	40	quarante	4 000	quatre mille
5	cinq	50	cinquante	1 000 000	un million
6	six	60	soixante	1998	mil(le) neuf cent quatre-vingt-dix-huit
7	sept	61	soixante et un		
8	huit	62	soixante-deux		
9	neuf	70	soixante-dix		
10	dix	71	soixante et onze		
11	onze	72	soixante-douze		
12	douze	73	soixante-treize		
13	treize	80	quatre-vingts		
14	quatorze	81	quatre-vingt-un		
15	quinze	82	quatre-vingt-deux		
16	seize	90	quatre-vingt-dix		
17	dix-sept	91	quatre-vingt-onze		
18	dix-huit	92	quatre-vingt-douze		
19	dix-neuf	100	cent		
20	vingt	101	cent un		

Ordinal Numbers

le premier	-	the 1st
le deuxième	-	the 2nd
le dixième	-	the 10th
le onzième	-	the 11th
le douzième	-	the 12th
le vingtième	-	the 20th

Note

1 There is no one word for 70, 80 or 90 in standard French.
2 'quatre-vingts' and 'cents' drop the 's' when followed by another number.
3 'mille' never adds an 's' unless it means 'miles'.
4 For dates, 'le premier' is the only ordinal number used. For all other dates, the ordinary number is used,
e.g.: le premier avril - 1st April   le vingt octobre - 20th October

EXERCICES

A Ecris les réponses, par exemple: un plus trois > 1 + 3 = 4

1 treize plus (+) dix-huit
2 quarante moins (-) deux
3 vingt-deux fois (x) trois
4 trois cent quatre-vingt-quatre divisé par (÷) huit
5 deux cent cinquante divisé par vingt-cinq
6 deux cent quatre-vingt-sept plus onze
7 dix fois douze
8 trois mille quatre cents divisé par deux
9 onze fois cent un
10 quatre millions moins dix-sept

B Ecris les nombres et les dates en mots:

1 23
2 34
3 45
4 56
5 67
6 74
7 87
8 98
9 186
10 299
11 1066
12 1997
13 1999
14 2 001
15 6 978 691
16 1st May
17 2nd June
18 10th August
19 21st September
20 30th December

PRONOUNS (1)

What are they?
Pronouns are words used to replace nouns.
By using **them** (pronouns), **you** (the reader) don't have to repeat **them** (these nouns) over and over again.
If you are still not sure what pronouns are, look at the highlighted words in the previous sentence; they replace the nouns in brackets.

What are they in French?

Singular			Plural		
je	-	I	nous	-	we
tu	-	you	vous	-	you
il	-	he/it	ils	-	they (masculine or mixed group of people or things)
elle	-	she/it	elles	-	they (feminine)
on	-	one, you, we			

Note
1 There are two words for 'you' in French:
tu - when you are talking to one person in a familiar way: a child, a friend, or a member of your family
vous - when you are talking to one person in a formal way: an adult or someone you are not on familiar terms with or when you are talking to more than one person (familiar or formal)
2 When you use any of the pronouns above, the ending of the verb which follows it will change (see Verbs, pages 15 - 39).
3 There are other forms of these basic pronouns (see pages 46, 50 - 51).

EXERCICES

A Remplace les pronoms par les bons substantifs:
1 **Il** ne peut pas aller au cinéma. — mon père / ma soeur / mes frères
2 **Elle** est très gentille. — mon prof / ma copine / mes parents
3 **Elles** aiment manger le couscous. — ma mère / mon oncle / mes copines
4 **Ils** ont faim. — Paul et Marie / Paul / Suzanne et Julie
5 **Nous** ne sommes pas intelligents. — Pierre et moi / Pierre et sa soeur / mes grands-parents

B Choisis la bonne phrase:
1 Pierre, are you hungry? — Tu as faim? / Vous avez faim?
2 Pierre and Sylvie, have you any fish? — Tu as du poisson? / Vous avez du poisson?
3 Mr Smith, where do you live? — Où habites-tu? / Où habitez-vous?
4 Sit down, gentlemen! — Assieds-toi! / Asseyez-vous!
5 Where do you come from, Michel? — Tu viens d'où? / Vous venez d'où?

C Remplace les mots soulignés par les bons pronoms:
1 Mon frère et moi allons au lycée.
2 Ma soeur est absente.
3 Le lapin est très mignon.
4 Notre grand-père est secrétaire.
5 Vos voisins étaient bizarres.
6 Sa tante sort tous les soirs.
7 Un de mes amis joue du piano.
8 Mon père et moi avons vu un gorille en Afrique.
9 Mes grands-mères ont toutes les deux quatre-vingts ans.
10 Où est-ce que les profs de français sont allés pendant les grandes vacances?

VERBS

What are they?

You **have** probably **wondered** what a verb **is**: it **is** a word which **tells** you what somebody or something **does** or **is**. If you **are** still not sure, **look** at the highlighted words which **are included** in this explanation.

THE PRESENT TENSE (1) : Regular Verbs

What is it?

In English there are several ways of talking about the present, e.g.: I play, I am playing, I do play

In French there is only one form of the present tense, e.g.: je joue

So 'je joue' means 'I play', 'I am playing', or 'I do play'.

How verbs change in the Present Tense

This page / section deals with **regular** verbs: this means that they always follow the same pattern.

How they work:

1 Look up the verb in a dictionary or word list: the form of the verb you will find is called the '**infinitive**'. In French, the infinitive ends in -er, -ir or -re, e.g.: jouer (to play) finir (to finish) vendre (to sell)

2 Take off the -er / -ir / -re ending, leaving you with what is called the stem, e.g.: jou- fin- vend-

3 Add the correct ending, e.g.:

		-er	-ir	-re
I	je	jou**e**	fin**is**	vend**s**
you	tu	jou**es**	fin**is**	vend**s**
he/she/it	il/elle	jou**e**	fin**it**	vend
one	on	jou**e**	fin**it**	vend
we	nous	jou**ons**	fin**issons**	vend**ons**
you	vous	jou**ez**	fin**issez**	vend**ez**
they	ils/elles	jou**ent**	fin**issent**	vend**ent**

Note

1 'aller' is the only -er verb which does not have regular endings (see page 18).

2 There are some -er verbs which have regular endings but make changes to the stem (see page 16).

3 Although most -ir and -re verbs are regular, there are some which do not follow the pattern above (see page 19).

EXERCICES

A Remplis les blancs **s'il le faut**:

1 Je jou... au golf.
2 Nous fin... le pique-nique.
3 Vous vend... des glaces?
4 Il jou... avec ses soeurs.
5 Tu fin... à quelle heure?
6 Vous jou... dans un orchestre?
7 Elle fin... ses devoirs.
8 Mes parents vend... de la poterie.
9 Qu'est-ce qu'on vend... ici?
10 Les cours fin... à trois heures dix.

B Traduis les phrases de l'exercice **A** en anglais.

C Traduis en français:

1 He is playing tennis.
2 They are finishing the picnic.
3 I sell stamps.
4 We are playing with the baby.
5 When does she finish?
6 Do they play in a team?
7 I am finishing my homework.
8 Do you (tu) sell milk?
9 He is finishing his exam.
10 She's playing this evening.

PRESENT TENSE (2)
More about -er Verbs

There are a number of -er verbs which, although they have the same endings as regular verbs, make changes to the stem.

1 Most verbs whose infinitives end in 'e' or 'é' + consonant + -er behave as follows:

acheter		(to buy)	compléter		(to complete)
j'achèt**e**	-	I buy	je complèt**e**	-	I complete
tu achèt**es**	-	you buy	tu complèt**es**	-	you complete
il/elle achèt**e**	-	he/she/it buys	il/elle complèt**e**	-	he/she/it completes
on achèt**e**	-	one buys	on complèt**e**	-	one completes
nous achetons	-	we buy	nous complétons	-	we complete
vous achetez	-	you buy	vous complétez	-	you complete
ils/elles achèt**ent**	-	they buy	ils/elles complèt**ent**	-	they complete

The 'e' or 'é' changes to 'è' before a silent ending (these are highlighted in the examples above).
Other verbs which do the same thing are: préférer - to prefer lever - to lift

2 Some verbs whose infinitives end in -eter or -eler double the consonant before an 'e' which is not pronounced, e.g:

jeter		(to throw)			
je jett**e**	-	I throw	nous jetons	-	we throw
tu jett**es**	-	you throw	vous jetez	-	you throw
il/elle jett**e**	-	he/she/it throws	ils/elles jett**ent**	-	they throw
on jett**e**	-	one throws			

Other verbs which do the same thing are: s'appeler - to be called épeler - to spell
il s'appell**e** - he is called j'épell**e** - I spell

3 Verbs whose infinitives end in -yer generally change the 'y' to 'i' before a silent 'e'.
Verbs whose infinitives end in -ayer do not always make the change from 'y' to 'i'.

envoyer		(to send)	payer		(to pay)
j'envoi**e**	-	I send	je pay**e**/pai**e**	-	I pay
tu envoi**es**	-	you send	tu pay**es**/pai**es**	-	you pay
il/elle envoi**e**	-	he/she/it sends	il/elle pay**e**/pai**e**	-	he/she/it pays
on envoi**e**	-	one sends	on pay**e**/pai**e**	-	one pays
nous envoyons	-	we send	nous payons	-	we pay
vous envoyez	-	you send	vous payez	-	you pay
ils/elles envoi**ent**	-	they send	ils/elles pay**ent**/pai**ent**	-	they pay

4 Verbs whose infinitives end in -cer require a 'ç' in the 'nous' form to keep a soft 'c' sound.
Verbs whose infinitives end in -ger require an 'e' after the 'g' to keep the soft 'g' sound.

e.g.:	commencer	(to start)	nous commençons	-	we start
	avancer	(to advance)	nous avançons	-	we advance
	manger	(to eat)	nous mangeons	-	we eat
	nager	(to swim)	nous nageons	-	we swim

EXERCICES

A Mets l'infinitif au présent:

1 Nous (acheter) des fleurs au marché.
2 Qu'est-ce que tu (préférer) comme sandwichs?
3 Qui (payer) le repas?
4 Tu (jeter) le ballon?
5 J'(envoyer) une lettre aux Etats-Unis.
6 Nous (manger) chez Philippe ce soir.
7 A quelle heure est-ce que le film (commencer)?
8 Je m'(appeler) Agnès.
9 Nous (commencer) à neuf heures moins vingt.
10 J'(acheter) des disques chez Virgin.

B Traduis en français:

1 He is called Peter.
2 I prefer egg sandwiches.
3 I am paying for the meal.
4 I throw the dice. (les dés)
5 We are sending a parcel to England.
6 I eat at twenty past nine.
7 We are swimming at Marie-Neige's house this evening.
8 We are advancing very slowly.
9 They prefer the cinema.
10 She is completing her studies at the university.

FLASH-INFO

To be good at French grammar, you have to learn to spot patterns in the language. You will not be expected to remember many exceptions to these rules, as long as you **communicate**.

PRESENT TENSE (3)
4 Irregular Verbs

In English, many verbs do not follow the same pattern as other verbs. We say these verbs are irregular,

e.g.:	to have:	I have, she **has**
	to be :	I **am**, she **is**

In French, irregular verbs are those which do not follow the same pattern as -er, -ir or -re verbs.
First of all, you must learn or revise the four most important verbs, each of which has to be learnt by heart. Even though they are irregular, you will see similarities between some of the endings of these verbs and regular verbs from the -er, -ir or -re groups.

<u>avoir</u>		(to have)	<u>être</u>		(to be)
j'ai	-	I have	je suis	-	I am
tu as	-	you have	tu es	-	you are
il/elle a	-	he/she/it has	il/elle est	-	he/she/it is
on a	-	one has	on est	-	one is
nous avons	-	we have	nous sommes	-	we are
vous avez	-	you have	vous êtes	-	you are
ils/elles ont	-	they have	ils/elles sont	-	they are

<u>aller</u>		(to go)	<u>faire</u>		(to do / make)
je vais	-	I go	je fais	-	I do / make
tu vas	-	you go	tu fais	-	you do/make
il/elle va	-	he/she/it goes	il/elle fait	-	he/she/it does / makes
on va	-	one goes	on fait	-	one does / makes
nous allons	-	we go	nous faisons	-	we do / make
vous allez	-	you go	vous faites	-	you do / make
ils/elles vont	-	they go	ils/elles font	-	they do / make

EXERCICES

A Mets l'infinitif au présent:

1 Je (être) dans la cuisine.
2 Nous (avoir) du fromage.
3 Il (faire) beau aujourd'hui.
4 Où (être)-tu?
5 Vous (aller) en ville.
6 Nous (être) très contents.
7 Ils (faire) de l'équitation.
8 Tu (avoir) des animaux?
9 Ils (avoir) beaucoup d'argent.
10 Je (aller) en France.

B Traduis les phrases de l'exercice **A** en anglais.

C Remplis les blancs:

1 Elle ..... à la discothèque. (go)
2 Nous ..... à la pêche. (go)
3 Vous .... un chat? (have)
4 Tu ..... du cyclisme. (do)
5 Ils ..... les cheveux roux. (have)
6 Je ..... anglais. (be)
7 Je ..... en ville cet après-midi. (go)
8 Elle ..... très petite. (be)
9 Ils ..... plus grands que moi. (be)
10 Qu'est-ce qu'ils .....? (do)

D Traduis les phrases de l'exercice **C** en anglais.

PRESENT TENSE (4)
Other Irregular Verbs

Irregular verbs do not follow the patterns of the three main verb groups (those with infinitives ending -er, -ir or -re).
On pages 55 - 57 you will find a list of all the irregular verbs you are likely to meet at GCSE / Standard Grade. You may wish to highlight the most important verbs or those that you come across. You should try to learn a few at a time.

Note

1 Although they are irregular, your task of learning these verbs will be made easier if you try to spot what they have in common.
The endings often follow this pattern:

je .....s or je x	nous .....ons
tu .....s or tu x	vous .....ez
il/elle/on .....t	ils/elles .....ent

2 Remember there is only one present tense in French,
e.g.:

je bois	-	I drink or I am drinking
nous lisons	-	we read or we are reading

EXERCICES

A Mets l'infinitif au présent. Sers-toi de la liste des verbes irréguliers aux pages 55 - 57.

1	Elle ..... une lettre à sa correspondante.	(écrire)
2	Je ..... mon pull quand il fait froid.	(mettre)
3	Je ..... aller en Italie après mes examens.	(vouloir)
4	Il ..... à la discothèque avec sa soeur.	(venir)
5	Tu ..... une limonade ou un coca?	(boire)
6	Je ..... la Tour Eiffel pour la première fois.	(voir)
7	Il est très intelligent, vous	(savoir)
8	Tous les jours à huit heures je ..... à l'arrêt d'autobus.	(courir)
9	Je ..... des magazines mais je préfère les BD.	(lire)
10	Le train ..... à onze heures dix.	(partir)
11	Nous ..... faire nos devoirs après l'école.	(devoir)
12	Je ..... dix livres par mois.	(recevoir)
13	Tu ne ..... pas venir?	(pouvoir)
14	Je ..... une douche à huit heures moins le quart.	(prendre)
15	Elle ..... la porte pour le prof.	(ouvrir)
16	Je suis malade: alors je ..... mal.	(dormir)
17	Il ne ..... jamais 'merci'.	(dire)
18	Lundi prochain nous ..... en vacances.	(partir)
19	Qui ..... la table?	(mettre)
20	Je ..... son numéro de téléphone.	(connaître)

B Traduis les phrases de l'exercice **A** en anglais.

C Traduis en français:

1 She wants to go to France after her exams.
2 I am writing a letter to my penfriend.
3 We are coming to the disco with her sister.
4 My father is reading the newspaper.
5 They are leaving at half past eleven.
6 I can come to the disco.
7 She must do her homework.
8 Do you know my father?
9 I lay the table. (mettre)
10 They drink coca-cola.

EXPRESSIONS WITH 'AVOIR' AND 'FAIRE'

A avoir

avoir ..... ans	-	to be ..... years old
avoir l'air	-	to appear (worried, etc.)
avoir chaud	-	to be hot
avoir envie de	-	to want to
avoir faim	-	to be hungry
avoir froid	-	to be cold
avoir horreur de	-	to hate
avoir lieu	-	to take place
avoir mal (à)	-	to hurt
en avoir marre de	-	to be fed up with
avoir peur de	-	to be afraid of
avoir raison	-	to be right
avoir soif	-	to be thirsty
avoir sommeil	-	to be sleepy
avoir tort	-	to be wrong

Note

Most of the verbs can be translated by 'to be' in English,

e.g.: J'ai chaud. - I **am** hot. Nous avons tort. - We **are** wrong. Il a seize ans. - He **is** 16.

B faire

faire attention	-	to be careful
faire de l'autostop	-	to hitch-hike
faire du bricolage	-	to do DIY
faire du camping	-	to go camping
faire les courses	-	to do the shopping
faire la cuisine	-	to do the cooking
faire des économies	-	to save up
faire les lits	-	to make the beds
faire le ménage	-	to do the housework
faire le plein	-	to fill up (with petrol)
faire une promenade	-	to go for a walk
faire du ski	-	to go skiing
faire du sport	-	to do / play sport
faire la vaisselle	-	to do the washing-up
faire de la (planche à) voile	-	to go sailing (windsurfing)
faire du vélo	-	to go cycling

Note

1 **faire** is often the equivalent of 'do', 'make' or 'go',
e.g.: Je fais de la planche à voile. - I am **go**ing windsurfing. Il fait le ménage. - He is **do**ing the housework.

2 **faire** is used to talk about the weather,
e.g.: Il fait chaud. - It is warm. Quel temps fait-il? - What's the weather like?

3 **faire** also translates 'to have something done',
e.g.: Elle fait nettoyer sa jupe. - She is **having** her skirt cleaned.
Mon père fait réparer sa Peugeot. - My father is **having** his Peugeot repaired.

EXERCICES

A Complète les phrases:

1 J' ..... tort.
2 Elle ..... du bricolage.
3 Tu ..... envie de sortir ce soir?
4 Il ..... froid à Skegness.
5 Je ..... des économies.
6 Nous ..... sommeil.
7 Il ..... mal à la main.
8 Tu ..... faim?
9 Le concert ..... lieu vendredi.
10 Est-ce que tu ..... réparer ton vélo?

B Traduis les phrases de l'exercice **A** en anglais.

C Traduis en français:

1 The match is taking place on Saturday.
2 I am sleepy.
3 They want to go out on Friday.
4 They are saving up.
5 Does your leg hurt?
6 We are thirsty.
7 She is having her skirt repaired.
8 What is the weather like in Nice?
9 I am hitch-hiking to London.
10 I am being careful.

THE PERFECT TENSE (1)
Regular Verbs with 'avoir'

What is it?

1 In French the perfect tense (le passé composé) is the most common past tense in everyday language. It is often used to talk about what somebody did in the past. It is useful for telling a story, rather than descriptions.

2 In English we use a range of past tenses to translate the passé composé,
e.g.: I helped, I did help, I have helped
I have helped is actually the perfect tense in English.

How to form the Perfect Tense of regular verbs

1 Use the form of the present tense of 'avoir' that you need (see page 18).

2 Form the **past participle** as follows:

a) Take the infinitive (see page 15), e.g.:	jouer (to play),	finir (to finish),	vendre (to sell)
b) Remove the -er/-ir/-re, leaving you with the stem, e.g.:	jou-	fin-	vend-
c) For -er verbs add -é, e.g.:	joué		
For -ir verbs add -i, e.g.:		fini	
For -re verbs add -u, e.g.:			vendu

The Perfect Tense of regular verbs in full

jouer	*(to play)*	finir	*(to finish)*	vendre	*(to sell)*
j'ai joué	*I have played*	j'ai fini	*I have finished*	j'ai vendu	*I have sold*
tu as joué	*you have played*	tu as fini	*you have finished*	tu as vendu	*you have sold*
il/elle a joué	*he/she/it has played*	il/elle a fini	*he/she/it has finished*	il/elle a vendu	*he/she/it has sold*
on a joué	*one has played*	on a fini	*one has finished*	on a vendu	*one has sold*
nous avons joué	*we have played*	nous avons fini	*we have finished*	nous avons vendu	*we have sold*
vous avez joué	*you have played*	vous avez fini	*you have finished*	vous avez vendu	*you have sold*
ils/elles ont joué	*they have played*	ils/elles ont fini	*they have finished*	ils/elles ont vendu	*they have sold*

EXERCICES

A Mets l'infinitif au passé composé:

1 J' .... le steak-frites. (choisir)
2 Nous ..... bien ..... (manger)
3 Qui .... les huîtres? (commander)
4 Ils .... des souvenirs. (acheter)
5 Elle .... la lettre samedi dernier. (envoyer)
6 Vous n'..... pas ..... mon cahier. (rendre)
7 Ils ..... déjà ..... leurs devoirs. (finir)
8 Mon père .... avec nous. (dîner)
9 J'..... ..... mes amis devant le cinéma. (attendre)
10 Cet été j'..... ..... des glaces. (vendre)

B Traduis les phrases de l'exercice **A** en anglais.

C Traduis en français:

1 She has chosen the omelette.
2 I ate well in France.
3 We have ordered some fish.
4 He bought ice-creams.
5 They sent the postcards last Friday.
6 I have given back the money.
7 You have finished your homework.
8 We had dinner at 8 o'clock in France.
9 He has waited an hour.
10 She sold the bike this summer.

THE PERFECT TENSE (2)
Verbs with être

There are 13 main verbs which use the Present Tense of 'être' (to be) rather than 'avoir' (to have) to form the Perfect Tense. Most of them can be learnt in pairs.

Infinitive	Meaning	Perfect Tense	Meaning
aller	to go	je suis allé	I have gone/I went
venir	to come	je suis **venu**	I have come/I came
entrer	to go in	je suis entré	I have gone in/I went in
sortir	to go out	je suis sorti	I have gone out/I went out
arriver	to arrive	je suis arrivé	I (have) arrived
partir	to leave	je suis parti	I (have) left
naître	to be born	je suis **né**	I was born
mourir	to die	il est **mort**	he (has) died
monter	to go up	je suis monté	I have gone up/I went up
descendre	to go down	je suis descendu	I have gone down/I went down
rester	to stay	je suis resté	I (have) stayed
tomber	to fall	je suis tombé	I have fallen/I fell
retourner	to return	je suis retourné	I (have) returned

Note

1 Another way of learning the verbs which take 'être' is by putting their initial letters together, e.g.:

D	**R**	**A**	**P**	**E**	**R**	**S**	**V**	**A**	**N**	**M**	**T**	**M**	**1**	**3**
e	e	r	a	n	e	o	e	l	a	o	o	o		
s	t	r	r	t	s	r	n	l	î	n	m	u		
c	o	i	t	r	t	t	i	e	t	t	b	r		
e	u	v	i	e	e	i	r	r	r	e	e	i		
n	r	e	r	r	r	r			e	r	r	r		
d	n	r												
r	e													
e	r													

2 The past participles of 'venir', 'mourir' and 'naître', highlighted in the list above, are irregular and need to be learnt.

3 Compound verbs of the above 13 - that is, verbs which look like them but add a bit - also take 'être',
e.g.: re**venir** - to come back, return r**entrer** - to go back, return (home)

4 The past participle of verbs taking 'être' must agree with the subject (whoever did the action). That is, it must add an -e for feminine, an -s for plural and -es for feminine plural.

e.g.:	je suis allé(e)	-	I went	nous sommes allé(e)s	-	we went
	tu es allé(e)	-	you went	vous êtes allé(e)(s)	-	you went
	il est allé	-	he went	ils sont allés	-	they went
	elle est allée	-	she went	elles sont allées	-	they went

Brackets round a letter mean it appears if necessary,

Alice: Je suis **allée** au supermarché. - Alice: I went to the supermarket.
Paul: Moi aussi, je suis **allé** au supermarché. - Paul: I went to the supermarket too.

EXERCICES

A Mets l'infinitif au passé composé:

1 Il .... au supermarché. (aller)
2 Nous .... à la boum. (venir)
3 Je .... en vacances le 1er août. (partir)
4 Elle .... aux magasins. (retourner)
5 Tu ..... jamais ..... à la Tour Eiffel? (monter)
6 Ma petite soeur .... lundi dernier. (naître)
7 Mes parents .... au lit. (rester)
8 Je .... de l'autobus au stade. (descendre)
9 Mon grand-père .... dans l'escalier. (tomber)
10 Mon hamster .... il y a un mois. (mourir)

B Traduis les phrases de l'exercice **A** en anglais.

C Traduis en français:

1 I went to the shops.
2 She came to the party.
3 They left for their holidays on 31st July.
4 We went back to the supermarket.
5 He got on the bus at the stadium. (monter dans)
6 I was born in Paris on 2nd December.
7 We arrived at the Eiffel Tower at half past one.
8 I went out after (the) dinner.
9 I went home after the football match. (rentrer)
10 I came back two months ago.

D Déchiffre les phrases:

	A	**B**	**C**	**D**	**E**
1	a	à	b	c	ç
2	d	e	è	é	f
3	g	h	i	j	k
4	l	m	n	o	p
5	q	r	s	t	u
6	v	w	x	y	z

1 D3, B2 / C5, E5, C3, C5 / A1, A4, A4, D2 / A1, E5 / B4, A1, B5, D1, B3, D2
2 B2, A4, A4, B2 / B2, C5, D5 / A6, B2, C4, E5, B2 / A1, E5 / D1, D4, A4, A4, C2, A3, B2
3 D3, B2 / C5, E5, C3, C5 / D5, D4, B4, C1, D2 / C5, E5, B5 / A4, A1 / E4, A4, A1, A3, B2
4 C4, D4, E5, C5 / C5, D4, B4, B4, B2, C5 / B5, B2, C5, D5, D2, C5 / B1 / A4, A1 / B4, A1, C3, C5, D4, C4
5 D3, B2 / C5, E5, C3, C5 / C4, D2 / B1 / A4, D4, C4, A2, B5, B2, C5

THE PERFECT TENSE (3)
Irregular Verbs

In English the past participle (see page 21) is not always regular: sometimes you have to learn it separately. For instance, we say 'I have walked' and 'I have followed' which have the regular '-ed' ending, but we also say 'I have made' and 'I have spoken', which do not follow the rules: they are irregular.
In French there are also irregular past participles. At the end of this book is a list of the irregular verbs you are likely to meet at GCSE or Standard Grade. Learn a few at a time! Some of the more common irregular verbs taking 'avoir' can be found below: learn them all.

Infinitive	Meaning	Perfect	Meaning
avoir	to have	j'ai eu	I (have) had
boire	to drink	j'ai bu	I have drunk/I drank
courir	to run	j'ai couru	I have run/I ran
devoir	to have to	j'ai dû	I (have) had to
dire	to say	j'ai dit	I (have) said
écrire	to write	j'ai écrit	I have written/I wrote
être	to be	j'ai été	I have been/I was
faire	to do	j'ai fait	I have done/I did
lire	to read	j'ai lu	I (have) read
mettre	to put (on)	j'ai mis	I (have) put (on)
ouvrir	to open	j'ai ouvert	I (have) opened
pouvoir	to be able	j'ai pu	I have been able/I was able/I could
prendre	to take	j'ai pris	I have taken/I took
recevoir	to receive	j'ai reçu	I (have) received
savoir	to know	j'ai su	I have known/I knew
voir	to see	j'ai vu	I have seen/I saw
vouloir	to want	j'ai voulu	I (have) wanted

EXERCICES

A Anagrammes:
1 J'ai **evuort** la porte d'entrée.
2 Il a **iaft** la cuisine.
3 Mon oncle a **ircét** une lettre.
4 Yannick a **uerç** un cadeau d'anniversaire.
5 Nous avons **idt** au revoir à nos profs.
6 Vous avez **rips** du thé.
7 Qui a **uv** Toy Story au cinéma?
8 Le voleur a **ruocu** comme un lapin.
9 J'ai **téé** en France à Pâques.
10 Elle a **sim** son manteau.

B Traduis les phrases de l'exercice **A** en anglais.

C Remplis les blancs avec le bon participe passé. Sers-toi de la liste en dessous de l'exercice:
L'année dernière j'ai ..... une bêtise. (something stupid) J'ai ..... de l'alcool et j'ai ..... un accident. J'ai ..... aller à l'hôpital. Lorsque mon père a ..... la nouvelle, il a ..... son anorak et il a ..... à l'hôpital. Il a ..... la porte et il m'a ..... J'ai dit, "Excuse-moi". J'ai ..... embrasser mon père.

bu / ouvert / couru / voulu / eu / dû / fait / mis / vu / reçu

D Traduis en français:
1 I ran like a hare.
2 We received a postcard.
3 He has done something stupid.
4 I have put on my coat.
5 They were in Italy at Easter.
6 He opened his (exercise) book.
7 The teacher said, "Stand up".
8 She had to go to the hospital.
9 We saw a comedy.
10 The thief took the radio.

THE FUTURE TENSE (1)

1 It is sometimes possible to use the Present Tense to talk about the future,

e.g.: **Je vais** en France l'année prochaine. - I am going to France next year.

2 A very common and quite easy way of talking about the future is to use the present tense of 'aller' (to go) followed by an infinitive (see page 15),

e.g.: **Je vais visiter** Paris en août. - I am going to visit Paris in August.

Here again is the Present Tense of 'aller' which you should relearn:

aller (to go)

je vais	-	I am going	nous allons	-	we are going
tu vas	-	you are going	vous allez	-	you are going
il/elle va	-	he/she/it is going	ils/elles vont	-	they are going
on va	-	one is going			

EXERCICES

A Complète les phrases avec la bonne forme du verbe 'aller':

1 Nous ..... acheter des cartes postales.
2 Je ..... boire un jus d'orange.
3 Elle ..... voyager en bus.
4 On ..... envoyer les résultats.
5 Tu ..... rentrer à la maison?
6 Vous ..... commander un steak?
7 Je ..... lire ce magazine.
8 L'autobus ..... partir à huit heures douze.
9 Il ..... être reçu à l'examen.
10 Nous ..... gagner le match de hockey.

B Traduis les phrases de l'exercice **A** en anglais.

C Traduis en français:

1 She is going to buy some postcards.
2 We are going to drink some coffee.
3 I am going to travel by bike.
4 They are going to eat some pizza.
5 I am going to go back home at quarter past four.
6 He is going to do my homework.
7 I am going to pass the exam.
8 Are you going to listen to some music?
9 They are going to leave.
10 I am going to swim in the sea.

D Déchiffre les phrases: Le weekend prochain .... (Code: b = a)

1 Kf wbjt sbohfs nb dibncsf.
2 Qvjt kf wbjt kpvfs bv gppu ebot mf qbsd.
3 Nbnbo wb mbwfs mb wpjuvsf.
4 Qbqb wb gbjsf mb dvjtjof.
5 Tbnfej tpjs nb dpqjof fu npj opvt bmmpot wpjs vo gjmn.

THE FUTURE TENSE (2)

As we have seen, French can sometimes use the Present Tense and very often use 'aller' followed by the infinitive to talk or write about the future. There is, however, a 'proper' Future Tense.

When is it used?
Obviously, to refer to the future (!), but it is more formal.

How is it formed?

A Regular Verbs:

manger		(to eat)	choisir		(to choose)	vendre		(to sell)
je manger**ai**	-	I shall eat	je choisir**ai**	-	I shall choose	je vendr**ai**	-	I shall sell
tu manger**as**	-	you will eat	tu choisir**as**	-	you will choose	tu vendr**as**	-	you will sell
il/elle manger**a**	-	he/she/it will eat	il/elle choisir**a**	-	he/she/it will choose	il/elle vendr**a**	-	he/she/it will sell
on manger**a**	-	one will eat	on choisir**a**	-	one will choose	on vendr**a**	-	one will sell
nous manger**ons**	-	we shall eat	nous choisir**ons**	-	we shall choose	nous vendr**ons**	-	we shall sell
vous manger**ez**	-	you will eat	vous choisir**ez**	-	you will choose	vous vendr**ez**	-	you will sell
ils/elles manger**ont**	-	they will eat	ils/elles choisir**ont**	-	they will choose	ils/elles vendr**ont**	-	they will sell

Note
1 Regular verbs add the endings to the infinitive, although -re verbs drop the final 'e'.
2 The above tense can be translated in two ways,
e.g.: je mangerai - I shall eat
and - I shall **be** eat**ing**

B Irregular Verbs:
Some verbs do not use the infinitive to form the future tense. They need to be learned separately. Here is a list of the most useful, but you will find more in the 'List of Irregular Verbs' on pages 55 - 57.

aller	(to go)	j'irai	-	I shall go
avoir	(to have)	j'aurai	-	I shall have
courir	(to run)	je courrai	-	I shall run
devoir	(to have to / to owe)	je devrai	-	I shall have to / I shall owe
envoyer	(to send)	j'enverrai	-	I shall send
être	(to be)	je serai	-	I shall be
faire	(to do / to make)	je ferai	-	I shall do / I shall make
mourir	(to die)	je mourrai	-	I shall die
pouvoir	(to be able)	je pourrai	-	I shall be able
recevoir	(to receive)	je recevrai	-	I shall receive
savoir	(to know)	je saurai	-	I shall know
venir	(to come)	je viendrai	-	I shall come
voir	(to see)	je verrai	-	I shall see
vouloir	(to want)	je voudrai	-	I shall want

Note
1 Remember, you can avoid the difficulty of forming this tense by using 'aller' + infinitive!
2 There are two quite important impersonal verbs (verbs used only in the 'it' form) which are also irregular:

il faut	-	it is necessary	il faudra	-	it will be necessary
il pleut	-	it is raining	il pleuvra	-	it will rain / it will be raining

EXERCICES

A Mets les phrases au futur:

1 Je regarde la télé.
2 Je travaille à New York.
3 Elle apporte du cidre.
4 Il voyage en train.
5 J'achète une glace.
6 Je téléphone à ma soeur.
7 Nous commandons des frites.
8 J'écoute de la musique.
9 Je retourne au magasin.
10 Elle me donne cent francs.

B Traduis les phrases de l'exercice **A** en anglais.

C Remplis les blancs:

1 Elle ..... une lettre. (envoyer)
2 Je ..... au tennis. (jouer)
3 Nous ..... la maison. (vendre)
4 Je ..... arriver après six heures. (pouvoir)
5 Tu ..... finir ton travail. (devoir)
6 Vous .....! (voir)
7 Je ..... à six heures moins le quart. (finir)
8 Ils ..... un cadeau à Noël. (recevoir)
9 Il ..... le ménage. (faire)
10 Je ..... un poster. (dessiner)

D Trouve la bonne réponse à chaque question:

1 Qu'est-ce que tu feras pendant les grandes vacances?
2 Est-ce que tu prendras l'hovercraft?
3 Tu iras avec tes parents?
4 Est-ce que tu visiteras Paris?
5 Tu logeras dans un hôtel?
6 Est-ce que tu nageras dans la mer?
7 Tu mangeras bien?
8 Est-ce que tu parleras français?
9 Tu enverras des cartes postales?
10 Quand est-ce que tu reviendras en Angleterre?

a) Oui, je prendrai des huîtres et des escargots.
b) Non, je prendrai le tunnel.
c) Je partirai le quinze juillet.
d) J'irai en France.
e) Non, j'irai tout seul.
f) Non, je n'écrirai rien.
g) Non, je resterai dans un camping.
h) Oui, j'apprendrai beaucoup.
i) Non, j'irai à Nice.
j) Non, je n'aime pas l'eau, mais je voudrais jouer au volley.

FLASH-INFO

The Future Tense is useful for talking about what you are planning to do after you leave school, and for saying what you are going to do on holiday.
Try preparing and recording talks on these two topics, using some of the verbs from the last three pages.

THE IMPERFECT TENSE

<u>What is it?</u>
The Imperfect Tense is a past tense.
It is used:

1 for descriptions of how things were,
e.g.: Sa nouvelle veste **était** orange et rouge. - His new jacket **was** orange and red.

2 for referring to repeated actions in the past,
e.g.: Je **prenais** le bus tous les jours. - I **used to** take the bus every day.

3 for speaking about things which continued over a period of time,
e.g.: Ils **allaient** en ville. - They **were** go**ing** into town.

So it is possible to translate the Imperfect Tense in more than one way,
e.g.: j'**allais** - I **went** <u>or</u> I **was** go**ing** <u>or</u> I **used to** go

<u>How is it formed?</u>
The Imperfect Tense is formed by taking the 'nous' form of the Present Tense (see pages 15 - 19), removing the -ons ending and adding other endings. Examples of the regular verbs are as follows (see next section for more information on meanings):

<u>finir</u>		(to finish)	<u>attendre</u>		(to wait)
je finiss**ais**	-	I was finishing	j'attend**ais**	-	I was waiting
tu finiss**ais**	-	you were finishing	tu attend**ais**	-	you were waiting
il/elle finiss**ait**	-	he/she/it was finishing	il/elle attend**ait**	-	he/she/it was waiting
on finiss**ait**	-	one was finishing	on attend**ait**	-	one was waiting
nous finiss**ions**	-	we were finishing	nous attend**ions**	-	we were waiting
vous finiss**iez**	-	you were finishing	vous attend**iez**	-	you were waiting
ils/elles finiss**aient**	-	they were finishing	ils/elles attend**aient**	-	they were waiting

But all irregular verbs (except one!) form the Imperfect Tense in the same way as the regular verbs above,

e.g.:	Infinitive	>	'nous' form of Present Tense	>	remove -ons ending	>	add other endings
	faire (to do / to make)	>	(nous) faisons	>	fais-	>	je fais**ais**, etc.

The only exception is 'être', whose Imperfect Tense is j'ét**ais**, tu ét**ais**, etc.

<u>Perfect or Imperfect?</u>
The Perfect Tense tends to emphasise that something **has been** completed: if you have **perfected** your French you needn't bother learning any more. (Unfortunately, this probably isn't true!)
The Imperfect Tense suggests that the action was still going on: if your French **was imperfect**, you had to **keep on** learn**ing**.

Compare:

<u>Perfect Tense</u>
Le weekend dernier, il a plu. - It rained last weekend.
At one specific time in the past (last weekend) it rained.

<u>Imperfect Tense</u>
Il pleuvait pendant le match. - It rained/was raining during the match.
The emphasis is on the fact that the rain lasted for a long time, or seemed to!

EXTRA-EXTRA-EXTRA-EXTRA-EXTRA-EXTRA-EXTRA-EXTRA-EXTRA-EXTRA-EXTRA-EXTRA-EXTRA

You can use the Imperfect and Perfect Tenses in the same sentence to say that something (one particular event) **happened** (Perfect Tense) while something else **was going on** (Imperfect Tense),

e.g.:	Imperfect	Perfect	Imperfect	Perfect
	J'écrivais une lettre quand	**il est entré**.	Il **était** dans la rue quand	**il a vu** l'accident.
	I was writing a letter when he came in.		He was in the street when he saw the accident.	

EXTRA-EXTRA-EXTRA-EXTRA-EXTRA-EXTRA-EXTRA-EXTRA-EXTRA-EXTRA-EXTRA-EXTRA-EXTRA

EXERCICES

A Mets l'infinitif à l'imparfait:

1 Je ..... la télé dans le salon. (regarder)
2 Nous ..... à l'arrêt d'autobus. (attendre)
3 Elle ..... des journaux en ville. (vendre)
4 Nous ..... le dîner à huit heures et demie. (finir)
5 Mon père ..... dans une usine. (travailler)
6 A Pâques mes parents ..... en France. (aller)
7 Tu ..... l'école avant moi. (quitter)
8 Hier soir, il ..... chez moi. (être)
9 J' ..... un chien. (avoir)
10 Qui ..... Take That?! (écouter)

B Traduis les phrases de l'exercice **A** en anglais.
Mais attention! Je regardais = I watched or I was watching or I used to watch or I would watch (regularly).

C Remplis les blancs avec un verbe à l'imparfait ou un verbe au passé composé:

1 Je ..... (lire) un livre, quand mon père ..... (téléphoner).
2 Quand elle ..... (descendre) du bus, il ..... (faire) froid.
3 La première fois que j'..... (voir) cet homme, il ..... (porter) la barbe.
4 Pendant que je ..... (manger) des sandwichs, un homme ..... (sonner) à la porte.
5 Nous ..... (chercher) son numéro de téléphone quand ils ..... (arriver).

D Traduis en français:

1 He was reading a book when I arrived.
2 When I got off the plane, it was very cold.
3 The last time you saw my father, you had a moustache.
4 While they were eating sandwiches, two men rang the doorbell.
5 You were looking for the phone number when I arrived.

THE PLUPERFECT TENSE

What is it?
The Pluperfect Tense is another past tense: it is a way of talking about something which happened before something else which also happened in the past.

How is it formed?
The Pluperfect Tense is one step further back than the Perfect Tense, so you need to use the Imperfect Tense of 'avoir' or 'être' (rather than the Present Tense), followed by the past participle,

e.g.:	J'**avais vu** mon frère.	-	I **had seen** my brother.
	Nous **avions garé** la voiture.	-	We **had parked** the car.
	Elle **était allée*** en ville.	-	She **had gone** into town.

* The past participle agrees in the case of verbs that take 'être' just as in the Perfect Tense. (See pages 22 - 23).

Examples of Pluperfect Tense in full:

Verb with 'avoir':		Verb with être:	
jouer	*(to play)*	aller	*(to go)*
j'avais joué	*I had played*	j'étais allé(e)	*I had gone*
tu avais joué	*you had played*	tu étais allé(e)	*you had gone*
il avait joué	*he/it had played*	il était allé	*he had gone*
elle avait joué	*she had played*	elle était allée	*she had gone*
on avait joué	*one had played*	on était allé	*one had gone*
nous avions joué	*we had played*	nous étions allé(e)s	*we had gone*
vous aviez joué	*you had played*	vous étiez allé(e)(s)	*you had gone*
ils avaient joué	*they had played*	ils étaient allés	*they had gone*
elles avaient joué	*they had played*	elles étaient allées	*they had gone*

EXERCICES

A Mets l'infinitif au plus-que-parfait.

1 Nous ..... très bien dormi.
2 J'..... mangé de la viande et des légumes.
3 Mon cousin ..... gagné le match.
4 Il ..... chanté une chanson anglaise.
5 Mes parents m'..... toujours aidé.
6 Nous l'..... invité à la surprise-partie.
7 Tu ..... oublié mon adresse?
8 Vous ..... réparé le pneu.
9 J'..... arrivé dans le train de 18 heures.
10 Ils ..... morts avant la deuxième guerre mondiale.

B Traduis les phrases de l'exercice **A** en anglais.

C Traduis en français:

1 I had forgotten your address.
2 She had arrived on the midnight plane.
3 He had always helped me.
4 I had slept very well.
5 We had won the match.
6 They had died in 1879.
7 They had sung a French song.
8 You had eaten fish and chips.
9 She had repaired the tyre.
10 I had invited him to the party.

THE CONDITIONAL TENSE

What is it?
The Conditional Tense is used to say what **would** happen if something else happened.

How is it formed in French?
If you know how to form the Future and Imperfect Tenses in French, you can form the Conditional Tense, because:
a) You take the stem for the Future Tense, e.g.: manger
b) and you add the Imperfect Tense endings, e.g.: je mangerais, etc.

1 Regular Verbs

	manger	(to eat)	choisir	(to choose)	vendre	(to sell)
je	mangerais	- I would eat	choisirais	- I would choose	vendrais	- I would sell
tu	mangerais	- you would eat	choisirais	- you would choose	vendrais	- you would sell
il/elle	mangerait	- he/she/it would eat	choisirait	- he/she/it would choose	vendrait	- he/she/it would sell
on	mangerait	- one would eat	choisirait	- one would choose	vendrait	- one would sell
nous	mangerions	- we would eat	choisirions	- we would choose	vendrions	- we would sell
vous	mangeriez	- you would eat	choisiriez	- you would choose	vendriez	- you would sell
ils/elles	mangeraient	- they would eat	choisiraient	- they would choose	vendraient	- they would sell

2 Irregular Verbs
These, too, take the same stem as for the Future Tense and add the Imperfect endings,
e.g.: je voudrais - I would like

How is it used?
a) Usually the Conditional Tense is used in complex sentences which contain a **si** ('if') clause.
However, the **si** part of the sentence uses the Imperfect Tense,
e.g.: Si j'**étais** riche, je **donnerais** de l'argent à tout le monde! - If I **were** rich I **would give** money to everyone!
b) It is commonly used to make requests in shops and restaurants,
e.g.: Je **préférerais** ces oranges-ci. - I **would prefer** these oranges.
Nous **voudrions** deux litres de lait. - We **would like** two litres of milk.
c) The Conditional Tense of **devoir** (to have to) can express the idea of 'ought' in English,
e.g.: Je **devrais** travailler pour mes examens. - I **ought** to work for my exams.

EXERCICES

A Mets les infinitifs au conditionnel ou à l'imparfait:
1 Si elle (pouvoir) chanter, elle (faire)* partie de la chorale.
2 Si tu (être) célèbre, tu (gagner) beaucoup d'argent.
3 Si j' (avoir) une voiture, je (pouvoir)* aller vous voir.
4 S'il (avoir) un emploi, il (rencontrer) plus de gens.
5 Nous (goûter) le vin, si nous (aller) en Italie.
6 Nous (vouloir)* habiter à Paris, si nous (pouvoir) trouver un appartement peu cher.
7 Ils (faire)* une excursion dans les Alpes, s'ils (avoir) le temps.
8 Ils (devoir)* apprendre le français.
9 Qu'est-ce que tu (faire)*, si je n' (être) pas là?
10 Je (vouloir)* changer cent livres sterling en francs français.

B Traduis les phrases de l'exercice **A** en anglais.

*Attention! Ces verbes sont irréguliers: sers-toi de la liste à la page 26.

REFLEXIVE VERBS

<u>What are they?</u>

These are verbs whose basic meaning suggests that a person or thing does something to **himself, herself** or **itself**,
e.g.: Je me lave. - I wash myself.
Of course, we usually say in English, 'I **get** washed'.

<u>The Present Tense of Reflexive Verbs</u>

<u>se laver</u>		(to get washed)		
je **me** lave	-	I get washed	nous **nous** lavons	- we get washed
tu **te** laves	-	you get washed	vous **vous** lavez	- you get washed
il/elle **se** lave	-	he/she/it gets washed	ils/elles **se** lavent	- they get washed
on **se** lave	-	one gets washed		

<u>Note</u>

1 The reflexive pronouns are highlighted above: they come in front of the verb.
2 **me**, **te** and **se** shorten in front of a vowel or a silent 'h'.

<u>Examples of the other main tenses</u>

Perfect:	Je me suis lavé(e)	- I got washed	Elles se sont lavées	-	They got washed
Imperfect:	Nous nous lavions	- We were getting washed			
Future:	Je vais me laver	- I am going to get washed	Ils se laveront	-	They will get washed
Pluperfect:	Il s'était lavé	- He had got washed	Ils s'étaient lavés	-	They had got washed

<u>Note</u>

Reflexive verbs take 'être' in the Perfect and Pluperfect Tenses. The past participle agrees in the same way as it does in the other tenses (see pages 22 -23).

<u>Daily Routine</u>

Many reflexive verbs are useful for describing what you do every day:

se baigner	-	to have a bath	s'habiller	-	to get dressed
se brosser les dents/les cheveux	-	to brush one's teeth/hair	se laver	-	to get washed
se changer	-	to get changed	se lever	-	to get up / stand up
se coiffer	-	to do one's hair	se mettre à	-	to begin
se coucher	-	to go to bed	se peigner	-	to comb one's hair
se dépêcher de	-	to hurry to do something	se reposer	-	to (have a) rest
se déshabiller	-	to get undressed	se réveiller	-	to wake up

<u>Other Common Reflexive Verbs</u>

s'amuser	-	to enjoy oneself	s'occuper de	-	to deal with
s'appeler	-	to be called	se présenter	-	to introduce oneself
s'arrêter	-	to stop (oneself)	se rappeler de	-	to remember to do something
s'asseoir	-	to sit down	se renseigner	-	to enquire
se blesser (le genou)	-	to injure oneself (one's knee)	se retourner	-	to turn round
se casser (la jambe)	-	to break (one's leg)	se souvenir de	-	to remember doing something
se couper (le doigt)	-	to cut (one's finger)	se tromper	-	to make a mistake
se demander	-	to wonder	se trouver	-	to be (situated)
s'excuser	-	to apologise			

EXERCICES

A Remplis les blancs avec le bon verbe. Sers-toi de la liste à côté de l'exercice.

Bonjour, je .....: je ..... Philippe.
Je ..... à sept heures et demie.
Je ..... dix minutes plus tard.
Je ..... les dents et ..... dans la salle de bains.
Après, je ..... dans ma chambre.
Puis, je ..... de mettre mes affaires dans mon cartable.
L'autobus ..... devant ma maison à huit heures vingt.
D'habitude je ..... les cheveux dans le bus.

me lave*	m'appelle	s'arrête*
me lève*	me brosse*	me brosse*
m'habille*	me dépêche*	me réveille*
me présente		

B Mets les verbes de l'exercice **A** marqués * au passé composé.

C Complète les phrases:

1	Bonjour, je ..... Je m'appelle Nicolas.	se présenter	-	présent
2	Il ..... de mon adresse.	se rappeler	-	passé composé
3	Elle	se changer	-	passé composé
4	Je ..... vers onze heures.	se coucher	-	futur
5	La voiture ..... aux feux rouges.	s'arrêter	-	passé composé
6	Manchester ..... dans le nord-ouest de l'Angleterre.	se trouver	-	présent
7	Nous ..... avant de partir.	se reposer	-	futur
8	Il ..... le bras dans l'accident.	se blesser	-	passé composé
9	Est-ce que vous ..... sur votre train?	se renseigner	-	passé composé
10	Il ..... souvent.	se tromper	-	imparfait

D Traduis en français:

1 We introduced ourselves.
2 I don't remember his address.
3 She is going to get changed.
4 I went to bed at about ten o'clock.
5 I stopped at the lights.
6 Paris is in the north of France.
7 We rested after the party.
8 I broke my leg in the accident.
9 I am finding out about my train.
10 I have made a mistake.

VERBS FOLLOWED BY AN INFINITIVE

In French, many verbs are followed by another verb in the infinitive form.
Remember: the infinitive is the form of the verb you find in a dictionary or word list; it ends in -er, -ir or -re,
e.g.: donner - to go finir - to finish rendre - to give back

Verbs followed by an infinitive without a preposition

Common examples:

aimer	-	to like to
aller	-	to go / to be going to
devoir	-	to have to (must)
entendre	-	to hear
espérer	-	to hope to
il faut	-	it is necessary to
préférer	-	to prefer to
pouvoir	-	to be able to (can)
savoir	-	to know how to (can)
vouloir	-	to want to
voir	-	to see

e.g.:	Je dois regarder le feuilleton ce soir.	-	I must watch the soap this evening.
	Tu sais nager?	-	Can you swim?
	Il aime marcher.	-	He likes walking.
	J'entends venir le facteur.	-	I can hear the postman coming.
	Je vais réussir.	-	I am going to succeed.

Verbs followed by **à** or **de** and an infinitive

Many verbs are followed by **à** or **de** and the infinitive. You cannot be expected to remember all of them at this stage, but here are some common ones.

1 à + infinitive

aider à	-	to help to
s'amuser à	-	to enjoy doing something
apprendre à	-	to learn to
arriver à	-	to manage to
chercher à	-	to try to
commencer à	-	to begin to
continuer à	-	to continue to
se mettre à	-	to start to
se préparer à	-	to prepare to
réussir à	-	to succeed in doing something

e.g.:	J'aide mon père à préparer les sandwichs.	-	I help my father to prepare the sandwiches.
	J'ai appris à jouer du piano.	-	I have learnt to play the piano.
	Il a commencé à faire le ménage.	-	He started to do the housework.

2 de + infinitive

arrêter de	-	to stop doing something
avoir besoin de	-	to need to
avoir envie de	-	to feel like doing something
avoir peur de	-	to be frightened of doing something
cesser de	-	to stop doing something
décider de	-	to decide to
demander de	-	to ask to
se dépêcher de	-	to hurry to
essayer de	-	to try to
finir de	-	to finish doing something
s'occuper de	-	to deal with
oublier de	-	to forget to
promettre de	-	to promise to
se rappeler de	-	to remember to
refuser de	-	to refuse to
se souvenir de	-	to remember doing something
venir de	-	to have just done something

e.g.: Nous avons décidé de vendre notre voiture. - We have decided to sell our car.
Est-ce que vous avez fini de parler? - Have you finished speaking?
Le prof a oublié d'apporter les livres.* - The teacher forgot to bring the books.

* Remember that **de** changes to **d'** before a vowel or silent 'h'.

EXERCICES

A Remplis les blancs **s'il le faut!**:

1 Il s'est mis ..... neiger.
2 J'ai commencé ..... manger mon dîner.
3 Elle a essayé ..... attraper le ballon.
4 J'ai continué ..... passer l'aspirateur.
5 Il a cessé ..... pleuvoir.
6 Je préfère ..... aller au centre ville.
7 Tu voudrais ..... lire le journal?
8 Je me prépare ..... participer au Grand Prix.
9 Nous venons ..... apprendre beaucoup de verbes.
10 J'ai besoin ..... aller aux toilettes.

B Traduis les phrases de l'exercice **A** en anglais.

C Traduis en français:

1 It stopped snowing.
2 I tried to do the hoovering.
3 I need to learn the verbs.
4 I am getting ready to eat my dinner.
5 It started to rain.
6 They continued to read the newspaper.
7 Would you like to go to the toilet?
8 He has just caught the ball.
9 She likes going to the town centre.
10 He's enjoying himself!

NEGATIVES

The negative (the opposite of positive!) can simply be 'non' in French (as opposed to 'oui'!) Unfortunately, you will not usually communicate enough with one word. Here is a summary of negatives in French:

ne ..... pas	-	not
ne ..... rien	-	nothing
ne ..... plus	-	no more, no longer, no ..... left
ne ..... jamais	-	never, not ..... ever
ne ..... personne	-	no-one, nobody, not anyone, not anybody
ne ..... que	-	only, not ..... until
ne ..... ni ..... ni	-	neither ..... nor
ne ..... aucun(e)	-	no ...., not any, none
ne ..... guère	-	hardly
ne ..... nulle part	-	nowhere, not anywhere

<u>Note</u>

1 Before a verb which begins with a vowel or a silent 'h', the word **ne** shortens to **n'**,
e.g.: Non, je **n'**aime **pas** les supermarchés. - No, I don't like supermarkets.

2 The **ne** ..... **pas** or other negative go on either side of the verb,
e.g.: Je **ne** vais **pas** à l'université. - I am not going to university.

3 **que** and **ni** are placed just before the word(s) they refer to,
e.g.: Je **ne** joue au golf **que** deux fois par mois. - I play golf only twice a month.
Je **ne** vais aller **ni** en France **ni** en Italie. - I am going neither to France nor to Italy.

4 In compound tenses (tenses which involve more than one word, e.g. the Perfect Tense), the negative goes before or after the first verb (the part of 'avoir' or 'être'),
e.g.: Nous **n'**avons **rien** mangé. - We ate nothing.
personne comes after the past participle,
e.g.: Ils **n'**ont vu **personne**. - They saw no-one.
ni, **que** and **aucun(e)** come before the word(s) they refer to,
e.g.: Je **n'**ai entendu **ni** mon père **ni** ma mère. - I heard neither my father nor my mother.
Je **n'**ai gagné **que** dix livres aujourd'hui. - I have only earned ten pounds today.
Le détective **n'**a trouvé **aucun** indice. - The detective didn't find one clue.

5 If the infinitive is being made negative, **ne pas**, **ne plus**, **ne rien**, **ne jamais** and **ne guère** come before it. The others wrap around it.
e.g.: J'espère **ne pas** échouer à l'examen. - I hope not to fail the exam.
J'ai décidé de **ne** voir **personne**. - I have decided not to see anyone.

6 **Personne** and **rien** can start the sentence when they are the subject,
e.g.: **Personne n'**a acheté mon livre. - Nobody bought my book.

7 Negatives can be combined in one sentence,
e.g.: Je **ne** comprends **plus rien**. - I don't understand anything any more.
Je **n'**aime **pas** les glaces **non plus**. - I don't like ice-cream either.

8 **un(e)**, **des**, **du**, **de la**, and **de l'**
change to **de** or **d'** after all negatives,
e.g.: Je **n'**ai **plus d'**oeufs. - I have no more eggs.
except **ne** ..... **que**,
e.g.: Je **n'**ai mangé **que du** pain. - I only ate bread.

EXERCICES

A Mets les phrases au négatif:

1 Je fais du vélo. ne ..... pas
2 Je vais aller en France. ne ..... jamais
3 Il mange des frites. ne ..... que
4 Je suis allé à la banque. ne ..... pas
5 Je suis allé en Italie. ne ..... jamais
6 J'ai entendu. ne ..... personne
7 Nous vendons des fleurs. ne ..... plus
8 Il espère trouver un emploi. ne ..... pas
9 J'ai décidé d'aller en France. ne ..... jamais
10 Ils ont donné des cadeaux à mon frère et à ma soeur. ne ..... ni ..... ni

B Traduis les phrases de l'exercice **A** en anglais.

C Mets les mots dans le bon ordre:

1 n' / je / pas / les / aime / sciences
2 n' / rien / il / au / achète / magasin
3 cent / que / n' / je / ai / francs
4 à / ne / école / l' / plus / va / elle
5 je / le / n' / jamais / ai / dessin / aimé
6 a / elle / personne / n' / vu
7 ne / ni / ni / je / à / ressemble / mon / père / à / ma / mère
8 de / ai / j' / décidé / n' / personne / inviter
9 joue / ne / je / piano / du / une / fois / qu' / mois / par
10 ai / n' / je / vu / part / mon / nulle / père

THE IMPERATIVE

What is it ?

The Imperative is a form of the verb used to give commands, instructions and make suggestions,

e.g.: **Go** home, please! **Work** harder! **Turn** the page.

In English it is easy, because we use the same form of the verb to speak to different people, since we have only one word for 'you'.

But remember, in French there are two words for 'you':

tu used to one person you know well, or to a young person (or animal!)

vous used to one person you address more formally, or more than one person.

How is it formed?

1 tu form:

Take the **tu** form of the Present Tense, e.g.:	tu finis	-	you finish
Remove the word **tu**, e.g.:	finis!	-	finish!

2 vous form:

Take the **vous** form of the Present Tense, e.g.:	vous finissez	-	you finish
Remove the word **vous**, e.g.:	finissez!	-	finish!

3 nous form:

Take the **nous** form of the Present Tense, e.g.:	nous finissons	-	we finish
Remove the word **nous**, e.g.:	finissons!	-	let's finish!

Exceptions

1 Regular -er verbs in the **tu** form remove the -s from the Present Tense,

e.g.: tu manges - you eat > mange! - eat!

2 Two other irregular Imperatives are:

	avoir		(to have)	être		(to be)
tu form	aie	-	have	sois	-	be ....
vous form	ayez	-	have	soyez	-	be ....
nous form	ayons	-	let's have	soyons	-	let's be ....

e.g.: Sois tranquille! - Be quiet!

N'ayez pas peur. - Don't be afraid.

Soyons courageux! - Let's be brave!

Note

Reflexive verbs have the reflexive pronoun after the verb,

e.g.: Tais-toi! - Be quiet! Levez-vous! - Get up! Dépêchons-nous! - Let's hurry!

EXERCICES

A Mets les phrases soulignées à l'impératif:

1 Vous allez à droite avant la gare.
2 Vous traversez le pont.
3 Tu tournes à gauche.
4 Tu vas tout droit.
5 Tu traverses la grande place.
6 Tu continues jusqu'au syndicat d'initiative.
7 Nous mangeons à huit heures.
8 Tu viens à la gare routière.
9 Tu mets ton anorak.
10 Nous restons à la maison.

B Traduis les phrases de l'exercice **A** en anglais.

C Mets les infinitifs à l'impératif:

1 (Attendre) à l'aéroport, s'il te plaît.
2 (Penser) à ta grand-mère, Paul!
3 (Aller) au supermarché, s'il te plaît.
4 (Prendre) la deuxième rue à gauche, monsieur.
5 (Tourner) à droite après l'hôtel, monsieur.
6 (Aller) à la discothèque! (nous)
7 (Partir) après le déjeuner. (nous)
8 (Continuer) tout droit, mademoiselle.
9 Ne (penser) pas à nous, monsieur.
10 (Aller), enfants de la Patrie .... (nous)
(La Marseillaise)

D Pour réussir aux examens! Déchiffre le code:

	A	**B**	**C**	**D**	**E**	**F**
1	A	B	C	D	E	F
2	G	H	I	J	K	L
3	M	N	O	P	Q	R
4	S	T	U	V	W	X

1 B4, F3, A1, D4, A1, C2, F2, F2, E1 / D1, C4, F3!
2 A3, A1, B3, A2, E1 / B1, C2, E1, B3!
3 B3, E1 / D4, A1, A4 / D3, A1, A4 / A1, C4 / F2, C2, B4 / B4, F3, C3, D3 / B4, A1, F3, D1!
4 F3, E1, A4, B4, E1 /C1, A1, F2, A3, E1
5 A1, A3, C4, A4, E1- B4, C3, C2!

ADVERBS

What are they?

Adverbs or adverbial phrases tell you **when**, **how** and **where** things are done,

e.g.:	**A deux heures**, je suis allé	**au travail**	**en voiture**.	-	At two o'clock, I went to work by car.
	when	**where**	**how**		
	time	place	manner		

Note

1 Many adverbs of manner (those which say **how** things are done) end in **-ment**: they are based on adjectives. As it is not easy to remember all the rules for forming adverbs of manner from adjectives, it is better to learn them individually,

e.g.:	absolument	-	absolutely	rarement	-	rarely
	énormément	-	enormously	régulièrement	-	regularly
	(mal)heureusement	-	(un)fortunately	vraiment	-	really, truly
	lentement	-	slowly			

2 Some adverbs of manner do not end in -ment,

e.g.:	bien	-	well	mieux	-	better
	mal	-	badly	vite	-	quickly

3 travailler **dur** - to work hard
Like 'hard' in English, **dur** looks like an adjective.

EXERCICE

A Anagrammes:

1 nieb
2 xeimu
3 tive
4 tlneement
5 ulosbament
6 miarvent
7 teramren
8 rehlamuseueemtn
9 lam
10 lugérièrenemt

COMPARISONS
Comparative Adjectives

What are Comparative Adjectives?
The comparative is used for comparing two people, objects, places or ideas. To do this we often use the Comparative Adjective.

How is the Comparative Adjective formed?
Examples in English: **more** interesting, **more** intelligent, young**er**, narrow**er**
In English, long adjectives have 'more' in front of the adjective, while shorter ones add -er to the adjective; but some are irregular,
e.g.: bad > worse
In French we use 'plus' instead of 'more' or an '-er' ending, unless the comparative form is irregular (see below).
e.g.: plus grand - bigger
In a sentence, French uses 'que' where English uses 'than',
e.g.: Il est plus grand que sa soeur. - He is bigger than his sister.
The adjective must still agree with the noun described, that is, it usually adds an -e if the noun is feminine and / or an -s if it is plural,
e.g.: **Elle** est plus intelligent**e** que son père. - She is cleverer than her father.

Other kinds of Comparison
Apart from the sentence pattern: plus ..... que - more ..... than,
there are other kinds of comparison,
e.g.: Il est **aussi** grand **que** moi. - He is **as** tall **as** me.
Elle est **moins** intéressante **que** moi. - She is **less** interesting **than** me.

Common Irregular Comparative Adjectives
bon (good) > meilleur (better)
mauvais (bad) > plus mauvais (worse: general)*
> pire (worse: when making a judgement on a person or a situation)*
e.g.: Mon travail de classe est toujours **meilleur** que mes devoirs.
My classwork is always **better** than my homework.
Le temps est **plus mauvais** aujourd'hui qu'hier.
The weather is **worse** today than yesterday.
Ne pas faire ses devoirs, c'est mauvais: mais recopier le travail d'un autre, c'est **pire**!
Not doing your homework is bad: but copying someone else's work is **worse**!

Comparative Adverbs

The examples above all use adjectives. It is equally possible to use adverbs when making comparisons between **how** two things are done,
e.g.: J'ai couru plus vite que lui. - I ran faster than him.

Common Irregular Comparative Adverbs
bien (well) > mieux (better)
mal (badly) > plus mauvais / pire (see* above)
e.g.: Elle joue **mieux** que nous. - She plays **better** than us.

Superlatives

What are they?
When comparing more than two people or things, we use the superlative.

How is it formed?
In English: the bigg**est**, the **most** intelligent, the **least** difficult
In French: **le**, **la** or **les** followed by **plus** (most) or **moins** (least)
e.g.: le plus grand bâtiment - the biggest building
The adjective must still agree,
e.g.: Elle est **la** moins intelligent**e** - She is the least intelligent.

Note
1 **le**, **la** or **les** is repeated when the adjective comes after the noun,
e.g.: **le** lait **le** plus frais - **the** fresh**est** milk
2 de translates 'in' after a superlative,
e.g.: Elles habitent la ville la plus historique **de** la France - They live in the most historic city **in** France.
3 Irregular superlatives: **le pire** - the worst; **le meilleur** - the best

EXERCICES

A Complète les phrases:

1. La voiture est .... que le vélo. (bruyant)
2. La voiture est .... que le train. (polluant)
3. La neige est .... la pluie. (amusant)
4. Les chips sont .... le saumon fumé. (cher)
5. Le coca est .... l'orangina. (cher: le coca: 9 francs; l'orangina: 11 francs)
6. La viande est .... le poisson. (cher: la viande: 48 francs; le poisson: 48 francs)
7. L'Empire State Building est .... la Tour Eiffel. (haut: L'Empire State Building: 448 m; la Tour Eiffel: 300 m)
8. La Seine est .... la Tamise. (long: La Seine: 145 km; la Tamise: 248 km)
9. La France est .... l'Angleterre. (grand: la France 549 000 km^2; l'Angleterre 130 000 km^2)
10. Paris est .... Londres. (ancien: Paris: fondé en 200 avant Jésus-Christ; Londres: fondé en 43 après Jésus-Christ)

B Traduis les phrases de l'exercice **A** en anglais.

C Réponds aux questions:

Prénom	Age	Taille	Maths	Anglais	Sport
Nicole	16	1,76 m	très bien	bien	très sportive
Isabelle	17	1,70 m	bien	très bien	sportive
Philippe	15	1,80 m	faible	bien	assez sportif

1. Est-ce qu'Isabelle est aussi sportive que Philippe?
2. Est-ce qu'Isabelle est moins grande que Nicole?
3. Est-ce qu'Isabelle est la plus forte en maths?
4. Est-ce que Philippe est plus fort que Nicole en anglais?
5. Qui est le plus âgé?
6. Qui est le plus grand?
7. Qui est le plus fort en maths?
8. Qui est le plus sportif?
9. Qui est le moins sportif?
10. Qui est le meilleur élève?

EXPRESSIONS OF QUANTITY

de (shortened to **d'** before a vowel or a silent 'h') is used after an expression of quantity,

e.g.:	un kilo **de** pommes	-	a kilo of apples	plus **de** fromage	-	more cheese
	un litre **d'**huile	-	a litre of oil	trop **d'**oranges	-	too many oranges

The following list contains the most common expressions:

500 grammes de	-	500 g of	moins de	-	less
(pas) assez de	-	(not) enough	un morceau de	-	a piece of
beaucoup de	-	a lot of	un paquet de	-	a packet of
une boîte de	-	a tin of / a box of	(un) peu de	-	(a) little / few
une bouteille de	-	a bottle of	plus de	-	more
une carafe de	-	a jug / carafe of	une portion de	-	a portion of
un demi-kilo de	-	half a kilo of	un pot de	-	a jar / pot of
un groupe de	-	a group of	une tasse de	-	a cup of
un kilo de	-	a kilo of	une tranche de	-	a slice of
un litre de	-	a litre of	trop de	-	too much / too many
une livre de	-	half a kilo (a pound) of	un verre de	-	a glass of

Note also:

quelque chose de	-	something	rien de	-	nothing .....

Some / Any

de and the definite article (**le**, **la**, **l'** and **les**) combine to form the word for 'some' or 'any' in French:

de + le =	**du**	e.g.:	du pain (nm)	-	some bread / any bread
de + la =	**de la**	e.g.:	de la limonade (nf)	-	some lemonade / any lemonade
de + l' =	**de l'**	e.g.:	de l'herbe (nf)	-	some grass / any grass
de + les =	**des**	e.g.:	des fromages (nmpl)	-	some cheeses / any cheeses

Note

The word for 'any' after most negatives is **de** or **d'** before a vowel or a silent 'h' (see Negatives, pages 36 - 37).

EXERCICES

A Trouve les paires:

1 une boîte de	a) vin
2 deux kilos d'	b) frites
3 un paquet de	c) bruit
4 une portion de	d) essence
5 un pot de	e) céréales
6 rien de	f) oranges
7 un groupe d'	g) bon
8 moins de	h) élèves
9 une carafe de	i) confiture
10 30 litres d'	j) chips

B Traduis les expressions de l'exercice **A** en anglais.

C Trouve le contraire de:

1 peu de fromage
2 plus d'eau
3 beaucoup d'amis
4 trop de gens
5 rien de difficile
6 trop de bruit
7 moins d'argent
8 pas assez de professeurs
9 beaucoup de succès
10 quelque chose d'intéressant

D Complète:

1 Vous voulez ..... fromage? (nm)
2 Avez-vous ..... pâtes?
3 As-tu ..... farine? (nf)
4 Est-ce qu'elle veut ..... beurre? (nm)
5 On a ..... huile.
6 L'enfant boit ..... lait. (nm)
7 Je voudrais ..... orangina.
8 Ils n'ont plus ..... cerises.
9 Donnez-moi un litre ..... huile.
10 Je préfère une tasse ..... thé.

QUESTIONS (1)
Introduction

There are different kinds of question in French.

A Questions may look like statements: if they are written down, only the question mark tells you they are questions, and if they are spoken, only the rise in your voice shows that you are asking something,
e.g.: Vous travaillez? - You work? Il a mangé son dîner? - He has eaten his dinner?

B Another way of asking the above questions is to put 'est-ce que' (is it that) at the beginning. The meaning does not change,
e.g.: Est-ce que vous travaillez? - Do you work?
Est-ce qu'il a mangé son dîner? - Has he eaten his dinner?

C Questions may also be formed by turning the subject (the person or thing doing the action) and the verb round (known as 'inversion'). This is generally used in formal language and with short verbs,
e.g.: Travaillez-vous? - Do you work? A-t-il mangé son dîner? - Has he eaten his dinner?

Note
1 A hyphen is inserted between the verb and the subject in this kind of question.
2 't' is also inserted if the verb ends in a vowel and the subject begins with a vowel.

D The above questions will get an answer which begins with 'Oui' or 'Non'. A more specific question, one asking for a time or a reason for example, can be asked by putting a question word or expression with any of the above three question types,

e.g.:	Vous travaillez où? Où est-ce que vous travaillez? Où travaillez-vous?	Where do you work?
	Il a mangé son dîner à quelle heure? A quelle heure est-ce qu'il a mangé son dîner? A quelle heure a-t-il mangé son dîner?	At what time did he eat / has he eaten his dinner?

The Most Common Question Words

Combien?	-	How much? / How many?	Qui?	-	Who?
Comment?	-	How? / What .... like?	Que?	-	What?
A quelle heure?	-	At what time? / When?	Qu'est-ce que?	-	What?
Quand?	-	When?	Quoi?	-	What? (usually after preposition)
Où?	-	Where?	Quel?*	-	Which?
D'où?	-	Where from?	Lequel?*	-	Which one?
Pourquoi?	-	Why?			

* These words change if what follows is feminine and / or plural,
e.g.: Quelle femme? - Which woman? Quels hommes? - Which men? Quelles filles? - Which girls?

QUESTIONS (2)
Examples

How?	Comment est-ce que tu viens au collège?	-	How do you get to school?
	Comment est ton collège?	-	What is your school like?
When?	A quelle heure est-elle arrivée?	-	At what time / When did she arrive?
	Quand va-t-il en vacances?	-	When is he going on holiday?
Where?	Où habites-tu?	-	Where do you live?
	D'où venez-vous?	-	Where do you come from?
Why?	Pourquoi est-ce que tu as choisi le français?	-	Why did you choose French?
How much / many?	Tu as combien de frères?	-	How many brothers do you have?
	Ça fait combien?	-	How much does that cost?
	Combien de fois as-tu rendu visite à Martin?	-	How many times / How often have you visited Martin?
	Combien de temps est-ce que tu passes devant l'ordinateur?	-	How much time do you spend in front of the computer?

'Who(m)' and 'what'

To understand the use of these question words, it is necessary to understand the meaning of the words '**subject**' and '**direct object**'. As we have already seen, the 'subject' of a sentence is the person or thing who does the action. The 'direct object' of a sentence is the person or thing affected,

e.g.: The cat ate the mat. 'The cat' is the subject, 'the mat' is the direct object.

Who(m)?	Qui a parlé?	-	Who spoke?
	Qui est-ce **qui** a parlé?	-	Who spoke? ('who' is the subject)
	Qui as-tu vu?	-	Who(m) did you see?
	Qui est-ce **que** tu as vu?	-	Who(m) did you see? ('who(m)' is the direct object)
	Avec **qui** est-ce que tu es allé au cinéma?	-	With who(m) did you go to the cinema? ('qui' is used with prepositions*)
What?	Qu'est-ce **qui** se passe?	-	What is happening? ('what' is the subject)
	Que faites-vous?	-	What are you doing?
	Qu'est-ce **que** vous faites?	-	What are you doing? ('what' is the direct object)
	Quel jour sommes-nous?	-	What day is it?
	Quelle est ton adresse?	-	What is your address?
	Comment?	-	What? (i.e., I didn't hear that, can you repeat it?)
	Quoi?!	-	What?! (informal exclamation)
	De quoi est-ce que tu parles?	-	What are you talking about? ('quoi' is used with prepositions*)

*See pages 47 - 49.

EXERCICES

A Remplis les blancs (sers-toi de la liste en dessous de l'exercice):

1 Avec .... vas-tu en vacances?
2 .... est ta soeur?
3 .... vas-tu au collège?
4 .... est dans le salon?
5 .... tu veux?
6 .... tu te lèves?
7 .... sport est-ce que tu préfères?
8 .... est-ce que tu vas aller en Espagne?
9 .... viens-tu?
10 .... est-ce que tu aimes l'équitation?

D'où / Pourquoi / Comment / Qu'est-ce que / Quel / Comment / qui / Qui / Quand / A quelle heure

B Traduis les questions de l'exercice **A** en anglais.

C Traduis en français:

1 When are you going to go to France?
2 What are you eating?
3 When do you eat?
4 Which teacher do you prefer?
5 Where does he come from?
6 How are you going on holiday?
7 Who is in the kitchen?
8 With whom do you go to school?
9 Why do you like swimming?
10 What is your mother like?

D Voici les réponses aux questions de l'exercice **C**!
Quelles phrases vont ensemble?

1 Je mange entre cinq et six heures.
2 Il vient d'Italie.
3 Parce que c'est bon pour la santé.
4 J'y vais avec mon petit ami.
5 Elle est généreuse et calme.
6 Mon cousin: il prend le petit déjeuner.
7 Je préfère le prof de dessin.
8 En aéroglisseur.
9 On part le deux mars.
10 Une tarte à la crème.

FLASH-INFO

Prof: Many students find it difficult to ask questions in French.
Élève: Comment?
Prof: A lot of students can't ask questions in French!
Élève: Pourquoi pas? We've got GRAMMAIRE ECLAIR!

PRONOUNS (2): Emphatic Pronouns

What are they?

moi	-	I / me	nous	-	we, us
toi	-	you	vous	-	you
lui	-	he / him	eux	-	they / them
elle	-	she / her	elles	-	they / them
soi	-	oneself			

When are they used?

1 Emphatic Pronouns always refer to people.

2 For emphasis!

3 After prepositions,
e.g.: Tu viens à la patinoire avec **moi**? - Are you coming to the skating rink with **me**?

4 Alone,
e.g.: Qui va payer l'addition? (Pas) **lui**! - Who is going to pay the bill? (Not) **him**!

5 After c'est / ce sont,
e.g.: C'est **moi**, Paul. - It's **me**, Paul.
Ce ne sont pas **elles**. - It isn't **them**.

6 In a comparison after 'que',
e.g.: Il est plus grand que **nous**. - He is taller than **us**.

7 With another noun or pronoun linked by 'et',
e.g.: Jeanne (**elle**) et **moi** allons au cinéma. - Jeanne (**she**) and **I** are going to the cinema.

8 With relative pronouns 'qui' and 'que' for emphasis,
e.g.: C'est **toi** qui as gagné! - **You** won! (literally, 'it is you who have won')

9 With 'aussi',
e.g.: Je voudrais une glace. **Moi** aussi! - I'd like an ice-cream. **Me** too!

10 With '-même(s)',
e.g.: J'ai pu le faire **moi-même**. - I was able to do it **myself**.

EXERCICES

A Traduis en français. Sers-toi de la liste des prépositions aux pages 47 - 49:

1 behind her
2 without him
3 against us
4 beside you (tu)
5 at my house
6 at his house
7 with them (two females)
8 for them (two males)
9 in front of you (the two of you)
10 between us

B Trouve et traduis les réponses:
par exemple: xx**sa**xx**ns**x**lu**x**i** = sans lui - without him

1 cxxhxezxtxoix
2 dxevxxaxntxluxi
3 sxaxnsxmxxoix
4 xxavxecxelxlxes
5 xpoxurxnxoxuxs
6 dxexrrxièxrexlxui
7 xcoxntxrexvoxusx
8 cxhexzxnxoxuxs
9 axxpxrèsxvoxxus
10 xxavxanxtexxlle

What are they?
A preposition is always placed (POSITIONED) in front of (PRE) a noun or a pronoun.
Examples in English: during, after, in, at, through, with.

Prepositions can refer to **place**, e.g.:	**behind** the bank
Prepositions can refer to **time**, e.g.:	**after** school
Some can refer to **place** and **time**, e.g.:	**in** the shop, **in** ten minutes
Prepositions can say **how** something is done, e.g.:	**by** bike

A Prepositions of Place

à	-	to, at, in (town, village, building)	derrière	-	behind
à côté de	-	next to, beside	devant	-	in front of
à droite de	-	to the right of	en	-	to, in (country, region, continent)
à gauche de	-	to the left of	en face de	-	opposite
au bout de	-	at the end of	entre	-	between
au fond de	-	at the end / bottom of	jusqu'à	-	as far as
chez	-	at .....'s house, shop, place	(pas) loin de	-	(not) far from
contre	-	against	près de	-	near (to)
dans	-	in	sous	-	under
de	-	from, of	sur	-	on (top of)

When **de** is followed by the definite article (**le**, **la** or **les**), you need to take care:

de + le	=	**du**	e.g.:	du marché	-	of the market / from the market
de + la	=	**de la**	e.g.:	à côté de la banque	-	next to the bank
de + l'	=	**de l'**	e.g.:	en face de l'hôtel	-	opposite the hotel
de + les	=	**des**	e.g.:	près des toilettes	-	near the toilets

When **à** is followed by the definite article (**le**, **la** or **les**), you need to take care:

à + le	=	**au**	e.g.:	au cinéma	-	to the cinema, at the cinema
à + la	=	**à la**	e.g.:	à la gare	-	to the station, at the station
à + l'	=	**à l'**	e.g.:	à l'hôtel	-	to the hotel, at the hotel
à + les	=	**aux**	e.g.:	aux feux	-	to the traffic lights, at the traffic lights

EXERCICES

A Traduis en français:

1 from the hospital (l'hôpital)
2 next to the butcher's (la boucherie)
3 near the lights (les feux)
4 not far from the houses (les maisons)
5 to the left of the bank (la banque)
6 to the right of the tourist office (l'office du tourisme)
7 beside the castle (le château)
8 a long way from the cinema (le cinéma)
9 near the bus stop (l'arrêt d'autobus)
10 from the school (l'école)

B Traduis en français:

1 at the theatre (le théâtre)
2 to the swimming pool (la piscine)
3 to the station (la gare)
4 at the baker's (la boulangerie)
5 to the motorway (l'autoroute)
6 at the church (l'église)
7 to the sea (la mer)
8 at the hotel (l'hôtel)
9 to the shops (les magasins)
10 to the park (le parc)

PREPOSITIONS (2)

Prepositions of Place: Some Difficulties Explained

1 **à** is used with the name of a town or village,

e.g.:	**à** Londres	-	to London, in London
	à Alva	-	to Alva, in Alva

2 **en** is generally used with the name of a country, continent or region,

e.g.:	**en** Angleterre	-	to England, in England
	en Afrique	-	to Africa, in Africa
	en Normandie	-	to Normandy, in Normandy

3 **au** is usually used with the name of a country when it is masculine,

e.g.:	**au** Canada	-	to Canada, in Canada

4 **aux** is used when the name of the country is plural,

e.g.:	**aux** Etats-Unis	-	to the United States, in the United States

5 **dans** is used with names of mountains,

e.g.:	**dans** les Alpes	-	to the Alps, in the Alps

B Prepositions of Time

à	-	at (.... o'clock)	depuis	-	for, since
après	-	after	il y a	-	ago
avant	-	before	jusqu'à	-	until
dans	-	in (length of time)	pendant	-	for, during
de ... à ...	-	from ... to	pour	-	for (future time)

Prepositions of Time: Some Difficulties Explained

1 in (time)

dans suggests **in** a certain amount of time from now,

e.g.: Je viendrai **dans** dix minutes. - I shall come in ten minutes.

en suggests **within** a space of time,

e.g.: J'ai fait mes devoirs **en** une heure. - I did my homework in one hour.

en is also used for months, seasons and years,

e.g.:	**en** février	-	in February
	en hiver	-	in winter
	en 1997	-	in 1997

Exception:

	au printemps	-	in spring

2 for (time)

depuis is used when you are talking about something which started in the past and is continuing.
If the English phrase uses the Imperfect Tense or the Perfect Tense, French uses the Present Tense.

e.g.: J'apprends le français **depuis** cinq ans. - I have been learning French for five years.

If the English phrase uses the Pluperfect Tense, French uses the Imperfect Tense.

e.g.: Il habitait en France **depuis** des années. - He had been living in France for years.

pendant suggests **for** or **during** a period of time in the past or future, but it is often left out,

e.g.: J'ai logé (**pendant**) deux semaines dans un hôtel. - I stayed in a hotel for two weeks.
Je serai absent (**pendant**) un mois. - I will be away for a month.

pour suggests **for** a pre-planned time,

e.g.: Je pars pour quelques jours. - I am going away for a few days.

3 since (time)

depuis means **since** a particular date.
If the English phrase uses the Imperfect Tense or the Perfect Tense, French uses the Present Tense.
If the English phrase uses the Pluperfect Tense, French uses the Imperfect Tense.

e.g.: Ma soeur est en France depuis le 1er mai. - My sister has been in France since 1st May.

C Other Prepositions

avec	-	with	par	-	by (someone, something)
de*	-	of	pour	-	for (someone, something)
en**	-	by (a means of transport)	sans	-	without

*for the use of **de** to mean 'belonging to', see page 11.

** **BUT** note: **à** pied - on foot

EXERCICES

A Remplis les blancs:

1 Je suis arrivé ..... Rouen.
2 J'habitais ..... Espagne.
3 L'année dernière il est allé ..... Canada.
4 ..... Windsor il y a un château.
5 ..... les Pyrénées il neige quelquefois en été.
6 Ils sont restés deux heures ..... parc (nm)
7 J'ai rencontré ma grand-mère ..... l'église.
8 Les toilettes se trouvent en face ..... la gare.
9 A Dieppe, le port n'est pas loin ..... magasins.
10 Il a couru un 100 mètres ..... 9,9 secondes.
11 Le dîner sera prêt ..... vingt minutes.
12 Les Jeux Olympiques auront lieu ..... 2 004.
13 ..... printemps il a fait très beau cette année.
14 J'habite ici ..... quatre ans.
15 Tu connais Paul ..... combien de temps?
16 J'ai habité ..... dix mois en Ecosse.
17 Je pars ..... huit jours.
18 Je serai absente ..... un mois.
19 Mon oncle va ..... le dentiste.
20 Nous avons visité nos amis ..... Normandie ..... une semaine. (a week ago)

B Traduis les phrases de l'exercice **A** en anglais.

PRONOUNS (3)

Subject Pronouns: see page 14.
Reflexive Pronouns: see pages 32 - 33.

Direct Object Pronouns
The following pronouns can be used only as the direct object of the verb, so **le** means 'him' or 'it' but never 'to him' or 'to it':

le - him / it   **la** - her / it   **les** - them

e.g.:	J'aime **le prof**.	- I like the teacher.	Je **l'**aime.	- I like him / her.
	Je déteste **le fromage**.	- I hate cheese.	Je **le** déteste.	- I hate it.
	J'ai mis **ma chemise**.	- I put on my shirt.	Je **l'**ai mis**e**.	- I put it on.
	Nous adorons **les fleurs**.	- We love flowers.	Nous **les** adorons.	- We love them.
	Je vais voir **les deux films**.	- I am going to see both films.	Je vais **les** voir.	- I am going to see them.

Note **1** These pronouns are placed before the verb, but note their position in the third and fifth examples above.
2 **le** and **la** shorten (to **l'**) before a vowel or a silent 'h'.
3 The past participle agrees with a direct object pronoun coming before the verb: so in the third example above, **mise** has an 'e' on the end because **l'** (it) refers to **ma chemise** (nf) (my shirt).

Direct and Indirect Object Pronouns
The following pronouns can be used as the direct object or the indirect object of the verb, so **me** means 'me' or 'to me':

me - (to) me   **te** - (to) you   **nous** - (to) us   **vous** - (to) you

e.g.:	Il **t'**a vu**e**, Mélanie!	- He saw you, Melanie!	(direct object)
	Il **m'**a offert une cassette.	- He has given a cassette to me.	(indirect object)
	Il **me l'**a offert**e**.	- He has given it to me.	(indirect object, direct object)

Note **1** These pronouns are placed before a verb.
2 **me**, **te**, **nous** and **vous** come before **le**, **la** and **les.**
3 In example 3 above, the past participle agrees with the direct object pronoun: it adds an **-e**.

Indirect Object Pronouns
The following pronouns can be used only as the indirect object of the verb:

lui - to him / to her / to it   **leur** - to them

e.g.:	J'ai donné ***la carte*** **à ma soeur**.	- I gave ***the card*** **to my sister**.	**Indirect Object**
	Je **lui** ai donné ***la carte.***	- I gave ***the card*** **to her**.	***Direct Object***
	Je ***la*** **lui** ai donné***e***.	- I gave ***it*** **to her**.	

Note **lui** and **leur** follow **le**, **la** and **les.**

y
y replaces **à** + noun (where the noun is not a person*),

e.g.:	Je vais **à la gare**.	- I am going **to the station**.
	J'**y** vais.	- I am going **there**.
	Elle pense **à son anniversaire**.	- She is thinking **about her birthday**.
	Elle **y** pense.	- She is thinking **about it**.

Note * where the noun is a person, **à** after certain verbs is followed by an Emphatic Pronoun (see page 46),

e.g.:	Je pense **à mon père**.	- I am thinking **of my father**.
	Je pense **à lui**.	- I am thinking **of him**.

en

en replaces **de** + noun (where the noun is not a person*),

e.g.:	J'ai besoin **de tomates**.	-	I need **tomatoes**.
	J'**en** ai besoin.	-	I need **them**.
	Je viens **de la gare**.	-	I am coming **from the station**.
	J'**en** viens.	-	I am coming **from there**.

Note *when the noun is a person, **de** is followed by an Emphatic Pronoun (see page 46),

e.g.:	J'ai besoin **de mes amis**.	-	I need **my friends**.
	J'ai besoin **d'eux**.	-	I need **them**.

SUMMARY OF WORD ORDER

Subject	**(ne)**	**me te nous vous**	**le la les**	**lui leur**	**y**	**en**	**Verb**	**Negative**	
Il	ne	m'					aime	pas.	He doesn't like me.
Je			le	lui			ai donné.		I gave it to him / her.
Tu	ne	t'				en	souviens	plus.	You don't remember (about it) any more.
Il	n'				y	en	a	plus.	There isn't / aren't any more.
Elle		me	l'				a donné(e).		She gave it to me.
	Ne		les				regarde	pas!	Don't look at them!

Note on the Imperative

1. In the negative there is no problem.
2. A positive instruction or command has different word order: pronouns follow the verb (see example for **4** below).
3. **moi** and **toi** are used instead of **me** and **te**,
   e.g.: Lève-**toi**! - Get up! / Stand up!
4. When two object pronouns are used, the direct object pronoun comes first,
   e.g.: Donne-**le**-**moi**! - Give it to me!

EXERCICES

A Remplace les mots soulignés par les bons pronoms:

1. Quelquefois, je trouve mes parents insupportables.
2. Je n'aime pas la chimie.
3. J'ai vu Angélique hier.
4. Est-ce que tu as regardé les informations? (nfpl)
5. J'ai parlé à ses frères.
6. Je ne pense jamais à mon travail.
7. Ma tante m'a envoyé cette carte d'anniversaire.
8. Vous n'avez pas répondu à la lettre.
9. J'ai peur des animaux.
10. Donne la raquette à Sylvie, s'il te plaît.

B Traduis en français:

1. Don't give it to him.
2. I like it. (le français)
3. I saw him today.
4. Did he see the match?
5. I never think about him.
6. They haven't replied to us.
7. We need it! (le courage)
8. She found it (la géographie) difficult.
9. The teacher watches me all the time. (toujours)
10. We sent a cheque to her.

CONJUNCTIONS

<u>What are they?</u>
Conjunctions are joining words,
e.g.: J'aime voyager **parce que** j'adore les langues. - I like travelling **because** I love languages.
Conjunctions allow you to progress from expressing yourself in simple sentences to linking ideas in longer, more impressive-sounding French.

It is a good idea to try to use some of the following in your speaking and writing:

aussi	-	so	après que*	-	after
car	-	for, because	dès que*	-	as soon as
donc	-	therefore, so	lorsque*	-	when
et	-	and	parce que*	-	because
mais	-	but	pendant que*	-	while
néanmoins	-	nevertheless	quand	-	when
ou	-	or	que*	-	that
où	-	where	si**	-	if, whether
pourtant	-	however			

* shortens to ....**qu'** before a vowel or a silent 'h'
** shortens to **s'** before 'il(s)'

e.g.: Je sais **qu'**elle est dans le bureau. - I know that she is in the office.
S'il y a un problème, demande de l'aide. - If there's a problem, ask for help.

EXERCICES

A Trouve la bonne conjonction.
Sers-toi de la liste en dessous de l'exercice:

1 Je voudrais aller en ville ..... il pleut.
2 Est-ce que tu veux nager ..... est-ce que tu préfères aller en ville?
3 Le collège est fermé ..... il a neigé hier.
4 Pierre prend un orangina ..... il lit le journal.
5 Je dois aller à la pharmacie ..... mon frère a mal à la gorge.
6 Je sais ..... il habite.
7 Je me suis endormi ..... j'étais dans le train.
8 Je pense ..... il est malade.
9 ..... il fait beau, nous allons faire un pique-nique.
10 J'aime bien jouer à la pétanque ..... j'adore faire du ski nautique.

et / ou / mais / pendant qu' / s' / parce qu' / qu' / quand / où / car

B Traduis les phrases de l'exercice **A** en anglais.

RELATIVE PRONOUNS

What are they?

In English: He is a man (**whom**) I admire. It is the same car (**that**) I saw yesterday.
It is the colour **which** is important. She is the person **whose** watch was stolen.
Jane, **who** lives round the corner, has just left you a message.

Relative Pronouns (**highlighted** above) link two pieces of information. In English they can sometimes be left out.

Examples in French

L'homme **qui** est entré est le voleur. - The man **who** came in is the thief.
L'accident, **qui** s'est passé hier, n'était pas grave. - The accident, **which** happened yesterday, wasn't serious.
L'homme **que** tu as vu est le voleur. - The man (**whom**) you saw is the thief.
L'accident **que** j'ai vu n'était pas grave. - The accident (**which**) I saw wasn't serious.

Note

1 **qui** and **que** are the main relative pronouns. They can refer back to a person, a thing or an idea.
2 **qui** is used when it is the subject of the verb, and **que** is used when it is the direct object of the verb (see page 44).
3 **qui** is never shortened, but **que** is shortened (**qu'**) before a vowel or a silent 'h',
e.g.: L'accident **qu'**il a vu n'était pas grave. - The accident (**which**) he saw wasn't serious.

Other Relative Pronouns

ce qui (subject) - what, e.g.: Je ne sais pas **ce qui** s'est passé. - I don't know **what** has happened.
ce que (object) - what, e.g.: Il ne voit pas **ce que** je fais. - He can't see **what** I'm doing.
dont - whose, of which, of whom
e.g.: J'ai beaucoup d'amis **dont** les parents sont divorcés. - I have lots of friends **whose** parents are divorced. (literally, **of whom** the parents .....)

After Prepositions

qui is usually used with people.
lequel / **laquelle** / **lesquels** / **lesquelles** are always used with things and ideas.
e.g.: Voilà la femme **avec qui** je travaille. - There is the woman **with whom** I work.
Voici le pont **sur lequel** il est passé. - This is the bridge **over which** he went.

où (where) is used :
a) for 'in' / 'to' / 'at' / 'on which',
e.g.: La ville **où** j'habite s'appelle Nice. - The town **where** (**in which**) I live is called Nice.
b) for 'when' after an expression of time,
e.g.: Je me souviendrai toujours du jour **où** je me suis marié. - I shall always remember the day (**when**) I got married.

EXERCICE

A Relie les phrases: remplace les mots soulignés par **qui** / **que** / **dont** / **où**.

1 J'ai deux frères. Ils ont trois et cinq ans.
2 J'ai un appartement. Je l'ai acheté l'année dernière.
3 Je connais une fille. Elle habite près de chez toi.
4 J'ai vu un homme. Je l'ai rencontré il y a deux ans.
5 Nous avons un balcon. Il donne sur le jardin.
6 Je partage un appartement avec un garçon. Il s'appelle Pierre.
7 Je porte souvent une robe. Sa ceinture est en cuir.
8 Voilà la femme. Son fils est dans ma classe.
9 J'ai un lapin. Je l'aime beaucoup.
10 Le restaurant est très cher. Nous allons y manger.

TIME

It is more common in French than in English to use the 24-hour clock.

12-hour clock	Meaning	24-hour clock	Meaning
il est ...	it is ...	il est ...	it is ...
une heure	one o'clock	une heure / treize heures	01.00 / 13.00
deux heures	two o'clock	deux / quatorze heures	02.00 / 14.00
neuf heures	nine o'clock	neuf / vingt et une heures	09.00 / 21.00
une heure dix	ten past one	une heure dix / treize heures dix	01.10 / 13.10
trois heures et quart	quarter past three	trois / quinze heures quinze	03.15 / 15.15
quatre heures vingt	twenty past four	quatre / seize heures vingt	04.20 / 16.20
cinq heures et demie	half past five	cinq / dix-sept heures trente	05.30 / 17.30
huit heures moins vingt-cinq	twenty-five to eight	sept / dix-neuf heures trente-cinq	07.35 / 19.35
neuf heures moins le quart	quarter to nine	huit / vingt heures quarante-cinq	08.45 / 20.45
midi	midday	douze heures	12.00
midi et demi	half past twelve (midday)	douze heures trente	12.30
minuit	midnight	vingt-quatre heures	24.00

Note

1 'demi' does not add 'e' after 'midi' or 'minuit'. Note also:
une demi-heure - half an hour

2 The following can be used after 12-hour clock times:
du matin - in the morning / a.m.
de l'après-midi - in the afternoon / p.m.
du soir - in the evening / p.m.

3 The following can be used before all clock times:
à - at (+ time)
vers - about (+ time)

EXERCICES

A Traduis en anglais:

1 sept heures et demie
2 onze heures et quart
3 dix heures moins le quart
4 midi moins onze
5 neuf heures trente-cinq
6 quinze heures six
7 vingt-deux heures quarante
8 dix-neuf heures quinze
9 huit heures trente-deux
10 vingt-trois heures vingt-cinq

B Traduis en français:

1 6 o'clock
2 half past ten
3 quarter to nine
4 27 minutes past 8
5 quarter to two
6 half past one
7 quarter past eleven
8 twenty to seven
9 five past three
10 midday
11 12.56
12 21.29
13 08.43
14 18.37
15 17.19
16 22.08
17 15.47
18 01.53
19 13.30
20 04.25

aller (to go)
Present
je vais
tu vas
il/elle/on va
nous allons
vous allez
ils/elles vont

Perfect
je suis allé
Imperfect
j'allais
Future
j'irai

s'asseoir (to sit down)
Present
je m'assieds
tu t'assieds
il/elle/on s'assied
nous nous asseyons
vous vous asseyez
ils/elles s'asseyent

Perfect
je me suis assis
Imperfect
je m'asseyais
Future
je m'assiérai

avoir (to have)
Present
j'ai
tu as
il/elle/on a
nous avons
vous avez
ils/elles ont

Perfect
j'ai eu
Imperfect
j'avais
Future
j'aurai

boire (to drink)
Present
je bois
tu bois
il/elle/on boit
nous buvons
vous buvez
ils/elles boivent

Perfect
j'ai bu
Imperfect
je buvais
Future
je boirai

conduire (to drive) *also: cuire (to cook)*
Present
je conduis
tu conduis
il/elle/on conduit
nous conduisons
vous conduisez
ils/elles conduisent

Perfect
j'ai conduit
Imperfect
je conduisais
Future
je conduirai

connaître (to know a person or place)
Present
je connais
tu connais
il/elle/on connaît
nous connaissons
vous connaissez
ils/elles connaissent

Perfect
j'ai connu
Imperfect
je connaissais
Future
je connaîtrai

courir (to run)
Present
je cours
tu cours
il/elle/on court
nous courons
vous courez
ils/elles courent

Perfect
j'ai couru
Imperfect
je courais
Future
je courrai

croire (to believe)
Present
je crois
tu crois
il/elle/on croit
nous croyons
vous croyez
ils/elles croient

Perfect
j'ai cru
Imperfect
je croyais
Future
je croirai

devoir (to have to; to owe)
Present
je dois
tu dois
il/elle/on doit
nous devons
vous devez
ils/elles doivent

Perfect
j'ai dû
Imperfect
je devais
Future
je devrai

dire (to say)
Present
je dis
tu dis
il/elle/on dit
nous disons
vous dites
ils/elles disent

Perfect
j'ai dit
Imperfect
je disais
Future
je dirai

dormir (to sleep)

also: s'endormir (to fall asleep)

Present
je dors
tu dors
il/elle/on dort
nous dormons
vous dormez
ils/elles dorment

Perfect
j'ai dormi
Imperfect
je dormais
Future
je dormirai

écrire (to write)

also: décrire (to describe)

Present
j'écris
tu écris
il/elle/on écrit
nous écrivons
vous écrivez
ils/elles écrivent

Perfect
j'ai écrit
Imperfect
j'écrivais
Future
j'écrirai

envoyer (to send)

Present
j'envoie
tu envoies
il/elle/on envoie
nous envoyons
vous envoyez
ils/elles envoient

Perfect
j'ai envoyé
Imperfect
j'envoyais
Future
j'enverrai

être (to be)

Present
je suis
tu es
il/elle/on est
nous sommes
vous êtes
ils/elles sont

Perfect
j'ai été
Imperfect
j'étais
Future
je serai

faire (to do; to make)

Present
je fais
tu fais
il/elle/on fait
nous faisons
vous faites
ils/elles font

Perfect
j'ai fait
Imperfect
je faisais
Future
je ferai

lire (to read)

Present
je lis
tu lis
il/elle/on lit
nous lisons
vous lisez
ils/elles lisent

Perfect
j'ai lu
Imperfect
je lisais
Future
je lirai

mettre (to put)

also: promettre (to promise) permettre (to allow)

Present
je mets
tu mets
il/elle/on met
nous mettons
vous mettez
ils/elles mettent

Perfect
j'ai mis
Imperfect
je mettais
Future
je mettrai

mourir (to die)

Present
je meurs
tu meurs
il/elle/on meurt
nous mourons
vous mourez
ils/elles meurent

Perfect
je suis mort
Imperfect
je mourais
Future
je mourrai

naître (to be born)

Present
je nais
tu nais
il/elle/on naît
nous naissons
vous naissez
ils/elles naissent

Perfect
je suis né
Imperfect
je naissais
Future
je naîtrai

ouvrir (to open)

Present
j'ouvre
tu ouvres
il/elle/on ouvre
nous ouvrons
vous ouvrez
ils/elles ouvrent

Perfect
j'ai ouvert
Imperfect
j'ouvrais
Future
j'ouvrirai

-TABLE OF IRREGULAR VERBS - TABLE OF IRREGULAR VERBS-

paraître (to appear)
Present *also:* *disparaître* (to disappear)
je parais
tu parais
il/elle/on paraît
nous paraissons
vous paraissez
ils/elles paraissent

Perfect
j'ai paru
Imperfect
je paraissais
Future
je paraîtrai

partir (to leave) *also:* *sortir* (to go out)
Present
je pars
tu pars
il/elle/on part
nous partons
vous partez
ils/elles partent

Perfect
je suis parti
Imperfect
je partais
Future
je partirai

pleuvoir (to rain)
Present
il pleut

Perfect
il a plu
Imperfect
il pleuvait
Future
il pleuvra

pouvoir (to be able to)
Present
je peux
tu peux
il/elle/on peut
nous pouvons
vous pouvez
ils/elles peuvent

Perfect
j'ai pu
Imperfect
je pouvais
Future
je pourrai

prendre (to take)
Present *also:* *comprendre* (to understand) *apprendre* (to learn; to teach)
je prends
tu prends
il/elle/on prend
nous prenons
vous prenez
ils/elles prennent

Perfect
j'ai pris
Imperfect
je prenais
Future
je prendrai

recevoir (to receive)
Present *also:* *décevoir* (to disappoint)
je reçois
tu reçois
il/elle/on reçoit
nous recevons
vous recevez
ils/elles reçoivent

Perfect
j'ai reçu
Imperfect
je recevais
Future
je recevrai

savoir (to know a fact)
Present
je sais
tu sais
il/elle/on sait
nous savons
vous savez
ils/elles savent

Perfect
j'ai su
Imperfect
je savais
Future
je saurai

venir (to come)
Present *also:* *se souvenir de* to remember; *devenir* (to become)
je viens
tu viens
il/elle/on vient
nous venons
vous venez
ils/elles viennent

Perfect
je suis venu
Imperfect
je venais
Future
je viendrai

voir (to see)
Present
je vois
tu vois
il/elle/on voit
nous voyons
vous voyez
ils/elles voient

Perfect
j'ai vu
Imperfect
je voyais
Future
je verrai

vouloir (to want)
Present
je veux
tu veux
il/elle/on veut
nous voulons
vous voulez
ils/elles veulent

Perfect
j'ai voulu
Imperfect
je voulais
Future
je voudrai

INDEX